Fearless and Free

Fearless and Free

The Adventures of Frances Forrester-Brown

Sara Richardson

authorHOUSE®

AuthorHouse™ LLC
1663 Liberty Drive
Bloomington, IN 47403
www.authorhouse.com
Phone: 1-800-839-8640

Published by AuthorHouse   08/23/2014

ISBN: 978-1-4969-2563-3 (sc)
ISBN: 978-1-4969-2561-9 (hc)
ISBN: 978-1-4969-2562-6 (e)

Library of Congress Control Number: 2014912312

Table of Contents

Foreword

Some called her the "Queen of the Central American Jungle." But we in the family called her Aunt Franc and we thought of her as a bit of a character. We never knew where her next letter would come from, whose home she would visit next, on which train or riverboat she might arrive, what new adventures she would relate. What we did know is that she would never be boring.

Franc was not famous in the usual sense. She didn't write a best-seller or create a spectacular work of art or launch a social movement or discover a cure for malaria. Yet her life was remarkable for a woman born the daughter of a Baptist minister in the deep South soon after the Civil War. It was a journey full of daring adventures, fueled by her eager curiosity and fearless spirit. Those who knew her along the way found her unforgettable. For those who didn't, this is your chance.

Franc had no children of her own so there are no direct descendants to tell her story. Her brother Tom's son, Hudson Strode, was a prolific author - a historian and biographer who was also famous for teaching others how to write but he left no descendants. Franc's two sisters, Sallie and Bess, had seven children between them and from them came fourteen of my generation, followed over time by the predictable geometric increase in family members. There are dozens of us by this time, including great, great, great nieces and nephews - and beyond. Any of them could probably do a more literate job as her biographer. But being lucky enough to have in my possession many of her letters, diaries, photos and other memorabilia and having a long time interest in Aunt Franc, I am giving it a try.

We did not see her very often, living many miles from western Kentucky where she spent much of her final few years. But as I grew up, I was fascinated by what I knew of her life. It seemed so exotic. She was always on the move - postcards arrived from New York, from Miami, from Mexico, from Ireland, from Chicago, from California. She must have been rich, we thought. It was a life that I, perhaps born restless, found intriguing.... faraway places ..... strange-sounding names.

Franc seemed to want her life to be remembered even if only by herself. I don't know when she started keeping diaries. The first ones we have date from 1897 when she began her life in Guatemala as a newlywed at age 28. They continue from that time until 5 years before her death. The ones she kept in Guatemala were large ledgers produced for the British colonial service and intended for keeping notes and financial records on business and government affairs.

After her husband's death in Guatemala, Franc continued to keep diaries, writing in small pocket sized datebooks. There are more than 40 of them. Some entries were written in pencil and are badly faded. Some dates are missing. Some entries are written in her private code and partially indecipherable. Even so, we have been able to put together a narrative that tells us her story as she moved from place to place after her husband's death - working as a practical nurse, as a file clerk, as a companion - keeping up her prolific correspondence - attending lectures and classes - dancing - visiting mediums - enjoying a variety of male companionship - being a faithful, loyal friend to many and a devoted sister to her siblings.

I have chosen to write this as a sort of "second-hand" memoir, basing it primarily on her own writings. This includes not only her diaries but letters she received from many friends and copies of letters she wrote to others, especially with regard to Guatemalan matters. There are also manuscripts she wrote for possible publication and articles that were written about her.

Franc's life spanned that time in history that we are accustomed to call "The Turn of the Century," the *fin de siecle*. Of course, now we are 14 years into yet another century and soon historians will find another way to express that unique period. It was a time of change at many levels. The Industrial Revolution was in full swing and factories of every kind thrived, immigrants from far away places arrived on American shores by the boatload, railways proliferated, automobiles and airplanes arrived on the scene. The poor largely remained poor - but the rich grew ever richer in that Gilded Age.

Changes may have been greatest of all for women. Though it was still a man's world and woman's place was still primarily in the home, new job opportunities for them were opening up. Women who wanted - or needed - to work outside the home did not have to toil in factories or go into domestic service. Now they could be trained as nurses or could learn to be "lady typewriters," working in business offices. Franc would work at both of those jobs - but she would also have experiences that few of either sex could claim. Her life in the Guatemalan jungles - far from civilized amenities, at the end of flooded rail tracks, in danger from earthquakes and hurricanes and wild animals - would repeatedly test her energy and endurance.

In putting together this story, I have been most interested in getting to know Franc, in learning how she came to choose a life that was so full of privations, hard work, and dangers. She had grown up in a well-to-do family in a thriving city. There is every reason to think she could have lived an exceedingly comfortable, even luxurious, life with a man who would have provided all that a well-bred young lady could desire. But Franc did not want that settled and predictable life. She wanted adventure - she yearned for the open road - she was endlessly curious. If there was hard work and loneliness and illness along the way, so be it! At one point in Guatemala, she wrote to a friend,

I prefer freedom to anything...

Adjectives to describe Franc are irresistible. Resilient - intrepid - courageous - passionate - energetic - entertaining - engaging - earthy - compassionate. Relatives who knew her in her lifetime were not always as smitten with her as I and sometimes found her to be a bit of a snob - or to have an "unfortunate disposition" - or to talk too much - or to laugh too much - to be, in short, just too much! She was a grand study in contrasts. She was a *fashionista* who hunted jaguars; a society club woman who could sleep on a table in a patient's dreary house; a lover of dancing and dining in grand halls who entertained hobos at a San Francisco mission; a compassionate caretaker of the sick and injured who was a Christian Scientist and didn't really "believe" in sickness; a pioneer who was also a party girl; a manager of banana harvesters who attended seances in darkened rooms.

Franc was truly a "woman for all seasons" - a woman in full. If this were a movie the images could be.....

    Franc dancing in a New York nightclub wearing an odd dress made of advertising posters and stamps.

    Franc riding astride a huge mahogany log on a truck in the jungle.

    Franc at a Mayan ruin taking aim at a wild boar with her Winchester rifle.

    Franc in her best finery at a dance at the Governor's palace in Belize.

    Franc on the deck of her launch on the Rio Dulce, loading bananas from the plantations along the shore.

    Franc wearily traipsing cold Manhatten streets, looking for a humble filing job.

    Franc climbing San Francisco's hills on the way to visit a medium.

    Franc doing taxidermy on a mole she had caught in her garden.

    Franc and her sister Sallie - old ladies now - laughing together at the kitchen table at Sallie's Kentucky farm.

Enjoy the show.

Frances Strode at 25

Chapter 1

A TROPICAL VOYAGE

As the sun rose on the morning of July 1, 1897, the yacht *Republic* lay off the coast of Santo Tomas, Guatemala. The waters of the Bay of Galvez lapped gently against her sides as the passengers awoke to another day of steamy tropical heat. As they arrived on deck, they were greeted with their expected shore view of lush tropical foliage. Palm trees swayed, bright flowering shrubs abounded and vines climbed every vertical surface. But they were not thinking of scenery; rather, they wanted their morning meal - their coffee, their tea, their eggs and fruit. They found nothing - no food, no cook, and not even any captain. A small crew remained on board but were refusing to work. Before the day was far gone, six policemen arrived from nearby Puerto Barrios and took them off to jail.

This was but one of many trials during the six-month voyage of Franc and William Forrester-Brown on the *Republic*. Having spent the first two years of their married life in Mexico as coffee planters, they were setting out on a new venture. They were off to harvest mahogany in the Central America jungles. Mr. Spencer, who had urged Will to join him in that business, was not yet present on the yacht but his wife and daughter Jane were - along with a crew that seemed to change by the hour. Mrs. Spencer was proving a difficult shipmate. Older and more experienced in the life of the tropics, she treated Franc alternately as a servant or as an irritating child. Franc, a young woman of 28 and of a decidedly independent nature, found her company more difficult to endure than runaway cooks, drunken sailors or the heavy winds that sometimes rocked the ship.

As the yacht lay for several days within sight of Santo Tomas, crew members and passengers made frequent trips there as well as to the larger port, Puerto Barrios, a short distance east, and to Livingston a few miles northwest to buy food and other provisions. There they also looked for a new cook. But it was never easy to find boats to take them back and forth. The waters of the bay were choppy and dangerous, especially for the small skiffs, pitpains or dories they had to use; trips ashore could be frightening experiences.

Mr. Spencer had wired Will to look for a house in Santo Tomas where they could store their goods while they continued on their voyage to Mexico. Will and Franc went ashore to investigate and found a possible place. After a long but fruitless search by the owner for a key, they all climbed through a window and were able to pronounce it suitable. They cleared matters with customs officers, who noted that the property belonged to W.F. Brown and family who were "immigrants going into the interior to farm." They moved their paraphernalia into the house; a few days later, they learned that most of it had been stolen.

Keeping an adequate crew was a constant challenge. The erstwhile captain was ready to return - but then he wasn't. Cooks came and "didn't suit" - and went. The engineer got so drunk on one of his visits ashore that he was rolling around in the sand. The steward was paid off after complaints from Mrs. Spencer; later he wanted to return and brought a charge against the yacht for unjust dismissal. Likewise, the sailors who had been arrested earlier for abandoning the ship brought a charge of $100 for unjust imprisonment. Dealing with officials on shore was fraught with misunderstandings. When Mr. Spencer eventually arrived, he was told by the British consul in Livingston that Will had used abusive and vile language to him. When Will confronted him, the consul denied that he had ever said such things and accused Mr. Spencer of lying.

Mrs. Spencer continued to behave erratically and order Franc about. One morning when the cook left early, the crew wanted to eat and demanded that Mrs. Spencer feed them. Of course she insisted that was not her job. Franc looked around and found that plenty of food had been cooked before the cook left but when she mentioned it, Mrs. Spencer berated her for interfering. Another day, Franc gave a sick sailor peppermints for his nausea but was told that she and Will must not give the crew medicine.

Franc's patience was being sorely tried. In her diary, she wrote that she was "madder than mad" and wanted to get a room on shore. One day she wrote:

> *I ironed three shirts and a shirtwaist and washed a pair of trousers and nearly made a zouave and only got abused or jumped on three times. ...... But I have to smile and be pleasant when I am feeling just the extreme. I do it for my darling....*

Franc held her tongue and did not quarrel with Mrs. Spencer but she was relieved when, on July 18, the yacht left Santo Tomas to make the short trip to Belize, British Honduras. The seas were rough and it took almost two days to cover the less than 40-mile distance. Almost everyone was seasick - the cook, crew members, Will, even Franc herself. She wrote.

> *I was never so sick in my life before.*

And as they waited offshore for a pilot to take them in, she wrote,

> *The trampiest lot anyone ever saw are aboard this yacht.*

The weeks they anchored off Belize proved a much needed respite. The British colony there was a pleasant place with a relatively civilized environment. They were able to go ashore and shop for clothes and other amenities, get their washing done, even meet some congenial companions. They went to the Polo Club, dined out, and enjoyed music and dancing. Franc noted that they met a "French count" at the hotel. Sometimes new friends they had made visited them on board the yacht. There was soon some easing of tensions with the Spencers and Franc was even "pampered" by them after a tiring day ashore. Evidently, the civilized environment of Belize and some breaks in their "togetherness" on the yacht had worked wonders for them all.

But all was not entirely calm. When some Spaniards who were hired to work in the mahogany camps came on board to get their advances, one of them began to play an accordian. Mrs. Spencer sent word immediately that that instrument was never to be played on board - whereupon the musician tore it into a dozen pieces and threw it overboard.

One day the Spencers went ashore and Will and Franc were left alone. Franc wrote,

> *We had such a nice time by ourselves... we went down and had lunch and some beer... then we put on our night clothes and sat on deck awhile and .. came to bed.*

Before long, there were more such days. Mr. Mitchell from one of the mahogany camps arrived in Belize and Will and Spencer met with him. They began to sign on men to work at the camps. Spencer decided to go up river with Mitchell and Mrs. Spencer went with him part of the way, leaving little Jane in Livingston with a friend. Franc and Will were finally alone on the *Republic.*

During this lull in their travels, Franc was able to pursue an activity that she enjoyed and often turned to - out of necessity, since she always wanted to dress well and often was on a low budget - but also, for solace. Sewing seemed to soothe and engage her throughout her life and, as they rested off Belize, she remade the yacht's flag, ripping stars and anchors from the old one to make a new design. She also made shirts and skirts and wrappers for herself.

By the end of August, they were ready to leave Belize and continue their voyage, sailing along the Mexican coast for several months before returning to Guatemala to begin their lives at a mahogany *finca* in the midst of a tropical jungle.

Franc reported these experiences in a diary she kept for two months in 1897. It is a foretaste of the 17 years Franc would spend in mahogany jungles and banana plantations on the banks of the Rio Dulce. Years later, back in the States, she recalled it as the happiest time in her life. As we shall see, she thrived on it, taking the heat, the mosquitoes, the torrential rains, the malarial fevers she suffered, the runaway workers, the corrupt officials, the loneliness, the privations and dangers of remote jungle life in stride. She seemed indomitable. When Will was no longer with her, she fought hard for her property and her position. Though she never wanted to leave her beloved tropics, she ultimately had to bow to the reality of being alone in a world that would not recognize a woman's ability to manage property - or even her right to own it. In 1914, Franc sailed away from her adopted land, never to return. Though she would live another twenty years, this Guatemalan sojourn would be the essential fact of her life - her great adventure, a peak that would never be reached again.

Chapter 2
THE PREACHER'S DAUGHTER

It was hardly the predictable life for a Baptist minister's daughter from a small town in the southern United States.

Franc's father, Eugene Strode, served several churches in Tennessee before arriving in Huntsville, Alabama, in 1854 to be pastor of the Enon Baptist Church. His father was James McGowan Strode (b1796), a hero of the Black Hawk War and a prominent lawyer in Kentucky during the time of Lincoln and Douglas. His mother was Mary Buck Parrish Strode (b 1801). Soon after arriving in Huntsville, Eugene met and married Sally Irby Martin, the daughter of Thomas Fuller Martin, a prominent landowner in Madison County. Thomas's father, John, had come to Huntsville from Fairfax, Virginia, in 1808 and built a large and impressive home on 80 acres of land on Monte Sano mountain.

The wedding of Eugene and Sally took place in Huntsville on September 4, 1854. During their next ten years there - a time that saw the tragic upheaval of the Civil War - three children were born to them. They were Charles, Thomas and Sallie (Sarah.).

In 1865, Eugene left the church in Huntsville. He served for a few months under the Home Mission Society in Edgefield, Tennessee, then moved to Springfield. Our heroine, Frances Clare (Franc), was born there on January 8, 1869, the fourth offspring of Eugene and Sally. She was followed in 1871 by another daughter, Elizabeth Erwin (Bess). Sadly, in September of that year, their father, Eugene, was thrown from a horse and died of his injuries. He was buried in Maple Hill cemetery in Huntsville. Sally was left a widow with five children, one of them still a young baby.

Though I have little information about this period, we can assume that the widow and children were able to rely on the support of the Martins and Sally and her children moved back to Huntsville. In one of the articles Franc wrote after she left Guatemala, she attributes her wanderlust to her early days on a Southern plantation.

> *I have been told that I persistently followed my dad on his visits*
> *to the quarters of the hands - through the tall corn and white cotton,*
> *when I was hardly able to toddle.*

She was probably remembering her grandfather, Thomas Martin, the plantation owner, and not her father, who had died when she was two. She soon lost also her mother, Sally, who died in 1880 when Franc was 11. Sally's life had been a sad one - she had buried not only her husband but her oldest son, Charlie, who had died of TB in 1878. The other children were still quite young and Tom, the surviving son, went to live with their father's brother, George Strode, in Cairo, Illinois. The three daughters - Sallie, Franc and Bess - made a longer, more adventurous move to Denver, Colorado, to live with their father Eugene's sister, Fanny Strode, who was married to one of Denver's early lawyers and real estate developers, John Q. Charles. It is there that Franc grew into a young woman, enjoying a life she often referred to as "privileged."

Denver in the 1870's was not far beyond a western frontier town. It was founded in the 1850's when gold was discovered at the base of the Rocky Mountains. Prospectors and fortune-seekers poured into the new settlement on the banks of the South Platte river on horseback, on foot, in covered wagons and sometimes pushing their possessions in a wheelbarrow. The settlement became known as Denver - named for the governor of the Kansas territory, James Denver. When a huge gold strike was discovered in Central City, people left in droves to try their luck but gradually they returned to Denver's mild climate and stayed to help build it as a western trade center.

There were several disasters to deal with in Denver's early years. In 1863 a great fire burned much of central Denver to the ground; a year later, a flash flood swept down Cherry Creek, causing a million dollars in damage; then an Indian War broke out, cutting supply lines and leaving Denver with only 6 weeks of food.

But Denver's young inhabitants were optimistic - they knew the town would thrive as soon as the transcontinental railroad reached them. It was a huge disappointment when it was re-routed through Cheyenne. But instead of giving up, the town leaders decided that if the railroad would not come to them, they would find a way to go to it. They launched a fund-raising campaign and, by 1870, the Denver-Pacific spur had been built. When, on June 24, 1870, the first train arrived in Denver there was much celebration. It was a new era, bringing residents and supplies, as well as tourists. The population soared from 4,729 in 1870 to over 35,000 in 1880. It also put Denver on the map as a tourist destination.

It was during those dynamic years that Sallie (18), Franc (11) and Bess (9) arrived in Denver to live with the Charles family. There they would have that privileged life Franc mentioned. John Charles was a highly respected lawyer and, eventually, a judge. He also built, in 1891, one of Denver's first multi-story office buildings, the Charles Building. They were among early Denver's leading citizens.

John and Fanny Charles had had a daughter who died when she was less than a year old. They then adopted a girl whom they named Maude and the three Strode sisters were raised along with her. There is little information available about the life of the girls as they grew up in Denver. Public schools were available and they may have attended those. However, as the nieces of such a prominent city leader as Judge Charles, they may have been educated at private schools or even have had a governess. Sallie, the oldest daughter (my grandmother) was able to study music and remembered attending concerts in Denver by such noted singers as Adelina Patti and Jenny Lind. There she married Charles Pennebaker in the early 1880's. Her younger sisters, Franc and Bess, attended, in their late teens, a boarding school for young ladies - Monticello Female Seminary in Godfrey, Illinois, later known as Monticello College. Franc's experiences at Monticello affected her strongly and were memorable throughout her life.

Chapter 3
MONTICELLO

The school Franc attended from 1886-1890 was founded in 1838 and was one of the oldest all-female colleges in America. It was chartered as Monticello Female Seminary - but it was not simply a finishing school, preparing girls for marriage and society. Its founder, Captain Benjamin Godfrey, believed that women had a vital role in building the growing nation. This belief may have had some connection with the fact that he himself had five daughters; at any rate, he was fond of saying that-

If you educate a man you educate an individual; educate a woman and you educate a whole family.

Godfrey had led a life that was full of adventure and had made and lost two fortunes before he was 40. He had been a ship captain and fought in the War of 1812 and engaged in trading operations both south of the border and on the Mississippi River. He finally settled with his family of five girls and three boys in Illinois in 1834, became a successful merchant and built the school in 1838. He greatly admired Thomas Jefferson and decided to name it for Jefferson's estate in Virginia.

As the first head of the school, Godfrey chose the Rev. Theron Baldwin, a graduate of Yale who was one of a group of men determined to bring religion and culture to the frontier - at that time, the area west of the Alleghenies. Baldwin succeeded in gaining national attention for the school. He insured that the curriculum include not only music, art and needlework but also courses in mathematics, natural sciences, history, philosophy, and languages.

However, the administrator who succeeded him was the one most remembered and most beloved by the students. Harriet Newell Haskell, a New Englander who had graduated from Mt. Holyoke College, led the school for 40 years, from 1867 to 1907. She is said to have been not only an educator but a vital, uplifting force to the students. She was also their sympathetic friend. Along with Baldwin, she was influential in establishing the fine reputation enjoyed by the school. Some believe that she haunts the school to this day, her presence being occasionally felt as a hand on the shoulder or as a faint whiff of lilac perfume in the library.

It was while Miss Haskell was there that Franc, at age 17, began to attend Monticello. At that time (1886), the program involved four years of study beyond the rudiments which were given, if needed, in Preparatory and Intermediate departments. The college catalog noted that:

> *Less time than this will not suffice. No college for young men pretends to graduate a class under four years. Young ladies need more time: for, in addition to a regular course, they are expected to devote considerable time to those branches termed ornamental.*

Whatever that meant...? Franc managed to graduate in the requisite four years so we can assume that she arrived with some grounding in arithmetic, grammar, geography, penmanship, history, Latin, reading, spelling and composition. As the course progressed, there were ever advancing classes in those areas as well as in the natural sciences (botany, chemistry, astronomy and geology), world history and languages (Latin, German, and French with Greek being "optional"). There was also required at each level of the program, a weekly course in composition and in Bible which, in the last year, included mental science, moral science, and Evidences of Christianity.

The catalog expressed lofty views of the educational process - which seem to need re-discovery by educators every few generations.

> *Education is not....a process of storing the mind with information merely but the cultivation and development of all powers of the body, mind and soul; the attainment of graceful vigor, the habit of systematic thought and correct moral action......It is not so much to fill the mind with knowledge, as to aid in the formation of those habits of patient thought and investigation that will enable it to add to its own store.*

The emphasis on Composition is especially noted in the catalog. Every Wednesday during the entire program was devoted to it and Franc evidently enjoyed and benefitted from it. Throughout her life, she was a prolific letter writer, kept a diary for more than 40 years and wrote a number of articles about her life in Guatemala - some published, some remaining only in manuscript form.

Franc as a Monticello student

While at Monticello, Franc was known as Fanny which seems to have been her family's nickname for her. Like most girls who first leave home for school, she relished her independence and the new experiences, finding each full of significance and worthy of strange souvenirs and memorabilia. There is a tattered scrapbook that she kept during her years there. It is full of notes, dance cards, concert and play programs, calling cards, buttons, locks of hair, bits of fabric, even a disintegrating cotton boll.

The memorabilia Franc saved had much more to do with parties, dances, plays, concerts and other forms of entertainment than with serious study. She was often in St. Louis which was the closest "big city" to Godfrey and a site for vaudeville performances and theater and concerts. Vaudeville evenings included:

> THE TWINS: *in their own Song, as sung with great success 100 nights in London, England, "I Wonder Who they Are."*
> PAPA DERVILLE: *in his descriptive song, "Thirty Days in Jail."*
> THE KERRY DANCE: *by the whole family.*
> THE FAMILY BRASS BAND: *Master Eddie, leader. Who has had the honor of appearing before the Marquis of Lorne and the Princess Louise, in his wonderful cornet solos.*

Franc also attended Boston Symphony concerts there.

There are programs from a variety of plays and concerts - at St. John's Club, the St, Anne's Guild, the Geneva Club and at Elitch's Gardens in Denver. There is a program from the Denver Athletic Club in which the "performances" featured were calisthenics rather than musical numbers. Another rather unexpected item was -

> *A Celebration of the opening of a number of new and important Industrial Enterprises at Decatur and New Decatur, Alabama.*

This event included speeches and an old fashioned Southern barbecue with a Basket Pic-Nic and inspection of industrial plants - oak tanning, charcoal iron blast furnace, horse-nail factory, car-wheel works. It was not Franc's usual cup of tea. Then again, she was probably as curious as a teenager as she was later as an adult.

There are dance cards from parties Franc attended - all mostly full. It is hard to tell if there was any particular suitor during this time but there are calling cards with such names as E.S. Collins (St. Louis), J.M. Calderwood (Denver), E.H Wilson - a Denver attorney, George Lederle, Fred D. Bond, E.P. Eppich, Sidy Veto. They danced the waltz, the polka, the comus, the waltz quadrille and the schottische.

A card from "Willie" in Denver indicated that he would be "faithful and true." There is a highly romantic and fanciful letter, sent by a swain who was working at the Anaconda Mining Company in Butte City, Montana. He evidently was lonely and wrote a sad and lengthy soliloquy - for which he apologized before saying farewell.

A portrait of the class of 1887 of the Pennsylvania Military Academy in Chester shows an x over the head of one H. Cunningham, the tallest of the uniformed young men. Another letter - from H.H. - tells her that he is enclosing the letters she requested (presumably from Franc to him) and confirms that he is engaged to someone else and hopes that he has her congratulations. Another note - writer unknown - has a similar message, returning all her letters. Yet he hopes that she will not entirely banish him from her mind.

Though most of the things Franc saved in her scrapbook were about plays, parties and concerts, a document called the Bell Card reminds us that she was otherwise living in a quite disciplined environment. It lists the times at which every act was performed from the Rising Bell at 6:25 AM to the Retiring Bell at 9:30. In between there was breakfast, divided by groups, then Prayers at 9:05. Then there were classes in specific 35 minute divisions until dinner at 12:45. In the afternoon there were more 35 minute divisions, with supper at 6. After supper there was Devotion and then more study or classes in the evening. At 9:30, the bell rang for retiring.

Several programs and a newsletter were saved from the Railroad Union Mission in Denver. This appears to be an interdenominational organization that provided Sunday School and gospel services and meals and assisted in finding jobs for people who attended. Franc was listed as one of about thirty teachers in the intermediate Sunday School division. It was a busy operation, open 6 days a week. An annual report she saved indicated that 405 had visited their reading rooms and 572 had received employment assistance in just one week. She seems to have been active with this group for several years, whenever she was in Denver.

Franc enjoyed poetry and there are several poems in the scrapbook, often cut from a newspaper. Some were humorous, such as "A Queer Girl."

> *She doesn't like study; tis seldom she tries*
> *It gives her the headache and weakens her eyes.*
> *But she'll dance like a sylph at the Veiled Prophets ball*
> *Forgetting she ever had headache at all.*

> *Embroidering her slipper her vision is clear;*
> *Now isn't that queer?*

She sometimes took a stab at writing poems herself. There is one called "Compositions" which begins:

> *Composition! that dreaded word*
> *Once more demands attention*
> *To shrink from it is so absurd*
> *For arises no prevention.*

There are several clippings about women and their place in the world. She pasted in a clipping that included "Tributes to Women". Such as:

> *A fashionable woman is always in love with herself.*
> *- Rochefoucauld.*
> *Handsome women without religion are like flowers without*
> *perfume. - Heine*
> *A woman may be ill-shaped, ugly, wicked, ignorant, silly, and*
> *stupid but hardly ever ridiculous. - Desnoyers*
> *Between a woman's "yes" and "no" I would not venture to stick*
> *a pin. - Cervantes*

And so on. She added in her own hand a quote from Cowley: "What is woman? One of nature's agreeable blunders." A poem she saved called "Women's Rights" reflected the general view of the time as to a woman's place - which, in the main, was somewhat subservient. But in her own life, she always showed a strong streak of un-feminine independence and was very far from submissive. Reflecting on her later experiences as a "practical" nurse in Guatemala and Miami, though, these phrases about women's "rights" may be prescient.

> *The right to dry the falling tear*
> *The right to quell the rising fear*
> *The right to smoothe the brow of care*
> *And whisper comfort in despair.*
> *The right to watch the parting breath,*
> *To soothe and cheer the bed of death.*

Far and away the most significant event that occurred when Franc was at Monticello was the famous fire of November 4, 1888. The 125 students were sleeping peacefully when they were roused and pulled from their beds and told to run for their lives. The fire had started in the basement below the kitchen and had burned for some time before being discovered. When smoke began to pour into the connecting dormitories, the teachers and older girls led the others to escape down the stairs. Frightened though they were and some dressed only in their nightclothes, the girls carried souvenirs of affection in the form of books, birds and letters. It is said that Miss Haskell stood at the exit to make sure they were decently dressed as they fled! They huddled in front of the building until all were reported safe and then were distributed among the neighbors in the town of Godfrey and nearby Alton.

In describing the fire, the <u>NY Times</u> reported that Miss Haskell was "almost crazed" by the tragedy; but, apparently, not for long. A printed letter from her, dated November 14, was mailed to the students assuring them that they would finish out the school year in temporary buildings that were being erected immediately. And a New Montcello would rise from the ashes - in the same style and under the same old trees. Franc kept this letter, with its personal handwritten note to her from Miss Haskell. In it, she urged Franc - who seemed to be waiting out the crisis in St. Louis - to come back whenever she chose and not to worry about buying books or bedding as she could negotiate better prices. Miss Haskell added:

> *Don't lose heart - or give up painting. It will never fail you in the long run and will do you a world of good.*

That is the first comment we find regarding Franc's art work. Although some of her creations have survived among family members, there is no mention by her of continuing to paint after her marriage. It seems to have been something she pursued while in school and as a young single woman in Denver. In the dozens of diaries she kept while in Guatemala and later in New York - in San Francisco - in Miami - in Memphis - she does not mention it and seems to have given it up - although we don't know when. Her artistic bent later had expression in her dressmaking and the decorating of her various homes. In Guatemala, she took up photography, using an early Kodak camera, and developed her own pictures.

Miss Haskell entered upon a vigorous campaign to raise money after the fire and the new Monticello was built, the cornerstone being laid in conjunction with the graduation ceremony of 1889, on June 11.

Franc included among her souvenirs an advertisment that seems to be a spoof of the Prohibitionist rallies that were occurring in a number of places in the late 19th century. This was supposed to occur on the campus there on Monday, Nov. 5. There was to be a march around the campus and the flyer ended with...

> *The star-spattered banner, no more may it wave o'er Republican head and Democrat knave.*

Franc noted that since the fire occurred, the march did not happen but she also commented:

> *It might be well to state in round numbers the prohibitionists that were to compose this grand rally. They consisted of the vast number of TWO.*

As we shall see, Franc would not have been one of them.

Eventually, in the early 20th century, the use of "Ladies Seminary" as part of the school's name was dropped and it became known as Monticello College. It remained a two-year school for women but by the end of the 1960's, it had gone the way of many single sex colleges and it closed in 1970. The Godfrey campus is now the home of Lewis and Clark Community College, a two year school with more than 8500 students. If Miss Haskell's ghost is indeed still wandering the grounds, she must feel quite lost - and tired!

Franc kept in touch with Monticello classmates throughout her life, attending alumni gatherings and corresponding with her old friends. But her time there ended with her graduation in 1890. Her younger sister, Bess, remained another year. As was typical for young ladies who had been "finished" in a boarding school, Franc returned to her family in Denver, there to await the arrival of a "Shining Knight" - or in her case, a Tipperary Irishman.

Chapter 4
HER WILD IRISH LOVER

Returning to Denver in 1892, Franc spent the next few years pursuing what she later referred to as a "bright social career." Denver, though not Chicago or New York, was a flourishing city with mining - gold, silver, lead - being the principal industry. The Cripple Creek mine was fabulously productive at that time. Real estate was booming. Her uncle had just built one of the first Denver office buildings. Her older sister, Sallie, had married Charles Beverly Summers Pennebaker who had moved to Denver from Cairo, Illinois, and had opened the Real Estate office of Estey and Pennebaker. When Grover Cleveland was elected president in 1892, there were parades and fireworks to celebrate the victory and much rejoicing in the household, where Charles was a loyal Democrat.

Public transportation was by horse car, cable car or stagecoach. The Pennebakers traveled by buggy and kept their horse, Old Maud, in a barn behind their house. Hitching posts and carriage stops were everywhere.

We are not sure exactly where Franc lived during this period. The Judge and Fanny Charles lived in a big house at the corner of 11th and Broadway. They had been guardians of the Strode daughters since their mother died in 1880 and Franc, as a young woman of marriageable age, probably lived with them. The Pennebakers lived in two places while in Denver. One was a small house at 1155 S. 15th St. but when their fortunes improved, due to the success of the Estey and Pennebaker firm, they moved to a larger place, 137 Irvington Place.

In the Riverside Cemetary in Denver are buried several of Franc's family members. There is Judge Charles himself, who died in 1912. There is also his wife, Fanny (Frances), sister of Franc's father. Also buried there is Franc's grandmother, Mary Buck Parrish Strode, who had moved to Denver from Kentucky to be with her daughter and died there.

What was Franc's life like in those years? Based on what we find in her scrapbook and on what we know of subsequent events, it was active and busy and included both fun and good works. We know that she loved to dance and was interested in music and theater. She also was frequently engaged in useful and altruistic works, such as the Railroad Mission, mentioned earlier. In Guatemala and in the States in later years she was rarely without a "cause," usually involving the sick or the poor and down and out.

It is probable that this period in Denver was the time when she picked up some of her medical knowledge. During the years she was in Guatemala, she was constantly called upon to treat wounds, ease malarial fevers, rid people of hookworm and handle all manner of other physical ailments. There is no indication that she had any sort of formal training but she may have volunteered and observed whenever the opportunity arose, acquiring skills along the way.

At this time, Franc was greatly concerned about her brother, Tom, who came to Denver from Cairo, Illinois around 1894, hoping the mountain air would help cure his tuberculosis. He and his family lived with the Pennebakers there and Franc must have visited often, helping with his care. His wife and young son, Hudson, came with him to Denver. Hudson, in his memoir, <u>The Eleventh House,</u> remembers - though he was younger than four at the time - his visit to the Pennebaker home and his father's death there at only 28.

Franc's nephew, Eugene, remembered that Franc and her younger sister, Bess, went to the Chicago World's Fair in 1893. Though we have no particular reason to believe that Franc knew about it, it was that event - sometimes known as the Columbian Exposition - that marks the "coming out" of nursing as a profession in the making. Organizers called it the World's Fair Congress on Hospitals, Dispensaries and Nursing. Perhaps it is just an interesting coincidence that Franc was in the vicinity at that time - but nursing is a consistent theme in Franc's life.

This is also probably the period when Franc did some of her painting, referred to in the letter from Miss Haskell at Monticello and evidenced in possessions that are in the family. There is a beautiful female angel seated on a mossy hillside, painted on a plate. It is pastoral and romantic, typical of the sort of thing young ladies did in this late Victorian era. Another painting, quite different, is a rather dark portrait of a large horse. It is probably Maud - a long-lived animal who went with the Pennebakers when they moved back to Kentucky and seems to have lived almost as long as Franc did.

According to portraits that remain, Franc in her twenties was a beauty. Her face was a perfect oval with a clear, smooth complexion and expressive brown eyes. Her nose was classic in shape, neither large nor small. She had many photographic portraits made through her life and perhaps her most distinctive feature was her mouth which was full and shapely but turned down slightly at the outer corners. She never smiled in her portraits and seems to have purposely emphasized this feature, giving her a serious - sometimes even severe - expression. It was something of a "no nonsense" look. As she aged, it was almost arrogant - at other times, she seems sorrowful. She was average in height, appearing to be about 5'6" and, as she grew older, had a tendency to gain weight. In middle age, she became quite obsessive about weighing herself and in her forties and fifties, hovered around 150 - a number which, when noted in her diary, elicited exclamations of "horrors, double horrors!" But at this time, in the 1890's, she was a slender girl with abundant hair that was a warm chestnut brown. There is a lock of her hair in her scrapbook. Even after all these years, we can see that it is thick and wavy with reddish lights.

In her photographs at various ages from 14 to 60, Franc's hair was often styled with a curl or two on the forehead. Perhaps she was modeling her appearance on "The Gibson Girl" - that lovely creature in the popular drawings of the day that portrayed the ideal American girl. During this period in Denver, Franc had ample opportunity to cultivate her personal style, which was rather regal. She had a very erect bearing and often wore fashionable dresses decorated with beading and ribbons and lace. Her hair was styled in upswept waves with a few curls around her face and often it was crowned with a large, elaborate hat decorated with feathers and flowers. Of course, during her years in the Guatemalan jungles she was more apt to wear her hair in a knot on top of her head or in braids and dress in divided skirts or native garments. But her fashion sense never really deserted her, as we shall see. During this period in Denver, it surely helped as she pursued what she referred to as "a bright social career."

But the career for which young ladies were groomed was Marriage and, sooner or later, the right man was sure to come along. No doubt there were plenty of suitors for a girl as beautiful and socially acceptable as Franc. But it seems that when William Forrester-Brown appeared, the others were left by the wayside. In several articles Franc wrote in later years, she talks about her wanderlust.

> *...a road, be it on land or sea, from my earliest memory held me entrapped in its web of mystery - its lure of uncertainty as to what the next step might reveal.*

The life that Will seemed to offer Franc spelled Freedom! and opened up new trails for her. She fell an easy mark to the man she often called her "wild Irish lover."

But who <u>was</u> William Forrester-Brown and how did he happen to be in Denver? One of Franc's nephews remembered that he was working for the <u>Rocky Mountain News</u> but there is no indication otherwise that he had ever been a reporter or writer. He had, however, led an adventurous (if not "wild"- we don't really know) life and he was indeed Irish. Will was from the area of Cashel in county Tipperary and his family was what was often called "landed gentry." They owned a small estate which was managed after Will left to see the world by his brother, John. There were also three sisters, one of whom had married while the other two remained single and lived on the estate. After being educated in London, Will made his way to India. Among Franc's memorabilia is a letter from a firm in Madras in 1893 informing Will that, due to financial difficulties, his services were being terminated. It was a kindly letter, full of hope that he will find something else soon. It is not clear what his services consisted of but he seemed to have been working on a coffee plantation.

With this life of Irish landed estates and colonial adventures, Will was certain to appeal to Franc's vivid imagination. He was a heaven-sent answer to her wish to escape the limitations of middle class social life and see the world. And since looks do indeed count, those also were present. Photographs show an attractive young man whose "seat" on a horse was widely admired. He was tall and slim - 6'2", she remarked in a letter to a friend - with a thick mustache, wavy auburn hair and a handsome face.

Will circa 1898, newly wed

He must also have been quite likeable. In his obituary, it was remarked that he was "open-hearted and magnanimous, sympathetic and cheerful, with an infectious gayety." Franc noted, at his death, that he was very popular, respected, and loved. In short, there was plenty of that old Irish charm! Who could resist?

We don't know how they met in Denver but we do have letters that Will wrote to Franc in March, April and May of 1894. Will seems entirely smitten. In March, he wrote, addressing "my darling Fannie." He spoke of lying awake at night, bathed in tears, thinking of the "loveliest girl I ever met." He seems to have feared that she was toying with him and jealousy was making him miserable.

You are to me the sweetest angel on earth and I know you are far too good to let my love simply amuse you....I will never do anything unworthy of your love.... I will love you for ever and ever and would gladly give my life for you.

By April, their relationship had progressed to a more comfortable level and he called her "my own darling Franc." He began by saying that he had accustomed himself to call her Franc but..

I <u>always</u> use the prefix Darling.

This suggests that it was during these post-Monticello years in Denver that Franc began referring to herself as Franc rather than Fanny. Perhaps she found the latter rather childish. Franc certainly seems to convey more strength and independence than Fanny and to better fit the person she perceived herself to be. Franc suggests the *personna* she created for herself - tramping through the jungle wearing a divided skirt and carrying a Winchester rifle - far better than Fanny, who might be a demure young lady with ringlets and an embroidery hoop in her lap. Even so, she was always a bit ambivalent about her image. In the articles she wrote about her Guatemala life, she could not quite resist referring to herself as a "slip of a girl" while, at the same time, managing a crew of banana cutters. It probably took some time for her family to get used to "Franc." Eventually, though, it became the only name she was ever called.

Will tried in this second letter to cheer Franc up as she had been feeling sad and worried about her brother's illness. She had also had her fortune told and he feared that might have made her anxious. He wrote news from his family in Ireland who had just recently made up a party to attend a race meeting.

How I wish you and I were of the party, the cream of gallant Tipperary turn out in their best. The hunting season finishes always with a race meeting. I know the course well and rode there last year.

This must have sounded like a delicious prospect to Franc. He went on to say that he was pleased when she finished her letter with love.

The oftener I hear it the better. I <u>never, never</u> will tire of you, darling. You must not think it. I'm sure you have no faults or *deficiencies, darling. You are the most perfect little angel that I ever met and I love you to distraction. How I would love to take you in my arms and kiss your sweet face and tell you all this.*

Will signed this letter,

Your own devoted Willie Boy.

A letter in May of 1894 was briefer and primarily concerned with Will's work and his impatience with a co-worker or employer. His and Franc's relationship had reached a more comfortable level. They may have been engaged by then. At least, they seemed to be discussing their future, as he noted:

I wrote to Mexico today.

We have no letters from Franc to Will during this period - or later, even - but she seemed an equally devoted lover, referring to him in her diaries and manuscripts as "my darling," "my friend," "my companion." She viewed their relationship as not only a marriage but as a journey - a great adventure - that they were embarking on together. She perceived them as partners in their life in the jungle, in mahogany camps and on banana boats on the Rio Dulce. That feeling stayed with her through the many ups and downs of their years in the tropics. She had wanted to be in on the pioneering from the outset.

It is not surprising that her family was aghast at her plan to marry Will and join him in the little-known, "uncivilized" countries to the south. Though Central America is a stone's throw away compared to India, it must have seemed as frightening, risky and uncertain to them as a trip half way around the world. She referred to her family in one of her articles as "conservative" and to herself as a "young, inexperienced, sheltered" girl. Yet, having traveled at a very early age from Alabama to Denver and growing up there on the edge of the western frontier, this is something of an exaggeration. And of course, her four years at Monticello had exposed her to friends from around the country, to teachers who opened new vistas, to ideas and ambitions beyond what she had known. Whatever she had experienced, she had become something of a rebel, a girl who liked to think for herself. She wrote that the life Will held out for her...

> *...spelled FREEDOM....freedom from the limitations of social life - the hampering burden of modern wearing apparel wished on unsuspecting humanity by Dame Fashion and her sly ally False Pride - and when their work is done they laugh up their sleeve at your discomfort - freedom from musty traditions, dogmas and creeds.*

Those words were written more than 20 years later - after her years in the jungle, after Will's death, after learning to live alone and support herself and, ironically, after spending many hours fashioning and being photographed in that modern wearing apparel she seemed to scorn. But they indicate that a strong motivation for her choosing Will in 1895 was a wish to be free of the expectations placed on her by an upper middle class family and milieu. She had a strong streak of contrariness and a need to push boundaries. Perhaps the experiences of her life - being orphaned at an early age, moving across the country to be brought up by distant relatives, attending a somewhat progressive boarding school - had encouraged what was probably her naturally independent nature.

But whatever her motivations were for marrying Will, Franc was clearly in love and, as we shall see, remained so through the many trials they were about to endure.

Franc's older sister, Sallie, had had a rather grand society wedding when she married Charles Pennebaker six years earlier in Denver. It was what one might expect for a niece of John Charles. Franc, instead, married Will quietly and modestly at the Pennebaker home in March of 1895. Was this unpretentious wedding her preference - or did Uncle John and Aunt Fanny Charles disapprove of her decision to marry Will and leave for unknown lands? There is almost no mention of them in her diaries and letters through the coming years, suggesting that there may have been a break in their relationship. Her true family became her sisters, Sallie and Bess, and their children.

Franc was 26 when she became Mrs. William Forrester-Brown and set out for Mexico. Her great adventure had begun.

Chapter 5
THEIR NEW COUNTRY

They began their life together in Mexico. Will's experience in India had been on a coffee plantation and when the opportunity arose, he felt ready to try what he had learned there on a new continent. Franc was his invaluable aide and they worked for a time in the vicinity of Orizaba in the state of Veracruz on Mexico's Gulf Coast.

We know little about this period of their lives as Franc had not yet started keeping the journals and diaries she wrote for the rest of her life. However, soon after they moved there, Franc began to hear from some of her Monticello friends who had formed a group that kept up with each other through "round robin" letters. They asked her to be part of the round and she was delighted to be included. They called themselves "The Susans." She wrote to them:

> *It is impossible for you to imagine how much pleasure a letter or any comunication from outside can afford me.*

Evidently they were living in a remote area where mail service was erratic, at best. To meet the mail carrier, they had to go by horseback, often through water. Neighbors were at least five miles away. There were very few English speaking people in the area. After writing that her sister Bess had recently married and visited her in Mexico, she added that Bess was expecting a little one. But, she added:

> *That will not happen to us as long as we are here in the jungle. There is no English-speaking doctor under 5 days away. When we first came here we both had fever. It took me three months to recover and feel normal. I think it was pure nervousness - knowing there was no doctor I could call.*

Franc told her friends about her marriage - how she happened to choose Will.

I am partial to foreigners. I have known a German from the Hague, an Englishman from Bristol, a Scotchman from Edinborough, a Norwegian and my husband - he has the best qualities of all three....His family still lives on the old family estate where I hope to live one day. His parents are Scotch but he is Irish - I like Irishmen best. Once lovers, always lovers. They treat their wives like queens. Nothing is too good for us..

She tried to comment on what each of the "girls" - Maud, Hat, Lil, Carrie were names she mentioned - had written before including her news from Mexico. She promised that she would try to send some bird feathers that one of them had asked for, but she had not had a chance to get a gun "her size." She remarked that she tired more easily there and added:

Mexico is truly the land of manana - conducive to a lazy, careless, easy life.

They remained in Mexico only two years. In an article about Franc that was written after she returned to the states years later, there is mention that this two-year effort in coffee growing was a "battle" and plagued with ill luck. The suggestion was that there was a blight in the coffee crop similar to what Will had experienced in India. In the same article (written by W. Livingston Larned for <u>Field and Stream</u>) it was noted that an interesting stranger appeared at their Mexican *finca* and suggested a new plan - that Will and Franc join him and his wife in the mahogany forests of Guatemala. As he talked about the numerous camps that existed and the scores of available natives to work in them, the project appeared to be a good prospect. Certainly it was a way out of their current difficulties and worth a try.

This "interesting stranger" must have been Mr. Spencer, he with the difficult wife, whom we met in our introduction. For Will and Franc, this new life would mean living in the jungle for most of the year with the luxuries of civilization and the companionship of other like-minded Europeans or Americans virtually absent. Though we don't know whether she realized it at the time, it would mean for Franc an almost total absence of female friends or acquaintances. But she and Will seem not to have hesitated long in their decision. As we have seen, they chartered the yacht, <u>Republic</u>, and set out to explore their new territory.

Guatemala

Though no larger than Ireland, Guatemala is a country of many contrasts - in climate, in geography, in inhabitants. There are volcanic peaks, steamy Pacific beaches, rolling hills, virgin rainforests, hot, impenetrable jungles, rushing rivers, placid lakes. Franc later wrote that someone, attempting to describe the topography to her, took a sheet of writing paper in hand, crushed it well, threw it on the table and said, "THAT is Guatemala." Devastating earthquakes have occurred throughout its history. The largest concentration of Mayan Indians in the world is there and there is a wealth of Mayan archaeological sites.

Traveling through by car or donkey, one moves in just a few hours from a desert-like landscape dotted with cacti to a placid river flowing though a ravine to a dense jungle rainforest teaming with predatory wildlife to the serene beauty of the highlands. The climate is tropical with a rainy season lasting from May to November and including impressive cloudbursts and flooding. Though the highlands can be cool with low humidity, the rainforest's steamy heat is exhausting and enervating.

Tourists who go to the country are most likely to visit the ancient capital, Antigua, with its spectacular earthquake ruins and splendid churches - or the charming villages around lovely Lake Atitlan in the highlands - or the Mayan ruins of the Petan such as Tikal - or the Indian market centers like Chichicastenango. The area where Franc and Will settled - the Caribbean coast to the east - has fewer enticements to offer. The coastline is short - no more than 20 miles or so - and, though there is water aplenty, white sandy beaches are missing. It does have, however, a large, beautiful, placid lake, Izabal, emptying into the aptly named Rio Dulce (Sweet River) which flows through a dramatic gorge down to the Caribbean.

This river figures heavily in our story of Franc. The Browns were never far from it while they lived and worked in Guatemala and traveling on it in a variety of boats was often their only way to get from the interior to the sea and back.

There are two major towns along the Caribbean coast; both are mentioned often in this story and one was the site of a house where Franc and Will lived for a time. Puerto Barrios to the south is the major Caribbean port, the terminus for a railroad that carried goods and people between the capital, Guatemala City, and the Bay of Amatique which empties into the sea. In the late 19th and into the 20th century, it was controlled by the United Fruit Company and the bulk of all Guatemalan trade passed through it. Franc mentioned it repeatedly in her writings, often calling it just "Port." They had to go there to embark on any voyage, either to the States or Europe; to get the train to Guatemala City; to meet visitors or pick up packages; to ship their mahogany and bananas.

The other town, Livingston, is a few miles north along the Bay at the mouth of the Rio Dulce and can only be reached by ferry or boat to or from Puerto Barrios. It is a very different place from the busy port - a laid-back town with a mixture of Ladinos and Mayan Indians and Caribs. The Mayan culture is much less prominent there than in the highlands to the west but the Caribs are unique to the area.

Guatemala's Caribbean coast with Lake Izabal

A black race found nowhere else in the country, they had originally come from the island of St. Vincent as a result of a slave rebellion there. Their appearance is more African than Latino, their culture has elements of voodoo and spirit-worship, their language is distinctive and the women are believed to speak a different language from the men.

Livingston, though not a large place, was the site of the British consulate for the area. When Will was appointed vice-consul in 1907, he and Franc were able to use the consul house and alternated between living there and at their Tameja plantation up the river

Flowing from Livingston into the interior, the Rio Dulce heads into a deep gorge, between sheer rock faces hundreds of feet high. In one of Franc's articles, she paused in mid-story to describe this "marvelously beautiful river."

> *It is the outlet of a lake, fifty miles long and eighteen miles across and a Golfete - little gulf - just nine miles from the coast. It has carved its channel through limestone cliffs which rise as much as three hundred feet above the water in some places, while its depth as it emerges from the canon, is ninety feet. These perpendicular walls are entirely covered with a dense growth except in a few places where the foliage seems not to have been able to get a footing, leaving great patches of white stone upon which strange and weird "pictures" seem to be, in a frame of deep green. These green walls are artistically and attractively draped with blossoming vines in various colors of yellow, lavender, pink, blue and white, in bas-relief on a background of mottled green, the darker shades predominating. There are the usual points of interest pointed out to the casual traveler. The first is the "devil's kitchen", the white stone seeming to be smoked up as from an imaginary kitchen fire. The next is the "devil's elbow," a very sharp turn. I have often wondered why so many freaks of nature are laid at the devil's door. But now we have a change - the next turn is announced as the "turn of the Virgin" and I have always wanted to ask just what her stunt was. Then comes the Nun - an heroic figure, black robed against the glistening white limestone...*

Then comes a widening of the river into the Golfete, a habitat of the sea-cow, or manatee. The forests along the shore are the home of monkeys, tapirs and even jaguars.

Upstream beyond the Golfete, just before reaching Lake Izabal, there is the forbidding but splendid Castillo san Felipe. This fort was built by the Spanish to keep out English pirates who used to sail up the river to steal supplies and harass the trains. From San Felipe the river enters the lake, the wide, serene Izabal - more than 200 square miles in size.

While in Guatemala Will and Frank owned several properties - usually referred to as *fincas*. Initially they built a home in the jungle area south and inland from Puerto Barrios, bordering Honduras. A narrow gauge railroad ran through the jungle from the port and about 50 miles inland they cleared an area in what was once a lake but had long been drained. They called the *finca* San Francisco. There were six mahogany camps out from the plantation including those at Amates, Gualan and Milagro. Quirigua, the site of ancient Mayan ruins, is nearby, reachable by the railroad. The area was shot through with streams and rivers, all necessary to the business of moving the huge logs down to the port. This jungle area was their home base for the next five years and the railroad their transportation from place to place. In addition to riding on the train, they also used handcars, pumping them along the tracks as needed. Otherwise, there were horses and mules and ox-drawn carts or boats on one of the many rivers. It was a primitive life. While there, Franc helped to manage the camps and the laborers, learned to shoot big game and small, fished in the alligator-infested streams and collected a menagerie of animals and birds to keep her company.

The period when Franc and Will lived in Guatemala is coincidental with the emergence of the political entity often referred to as a "banana republic." It was during their time there that the United Fruit Company acquired vast tracts of land on the Atlantic coast and with them, their immense influence in Central America for the next few decades. This acquisition was made possible by the volatile and ever-changing nature of the political situation. The growing importance of the banana trade encouraged Will and Franc to purchase the land along the Rio Dulce that would become their banana plantation, Tameja.

Guatemala was for thousands of years prior to the 16th century Spanish conquest a Mayan civilization. Hundreds of cities were established and flourished but most were abandoned by 1000 AD. A Spanish conquistador, Pedro de Alvarado, arrived in Central America in 1525 and conquered most of the area for Spain where it remained part of the empire until 1821. Then, briefly, Guatemala was part of the First Mexican Empire and following that, was part of a federation called the United Provinces of Central America. Rafael Carrera led in breaking apart this union and dominated Guatemalan politics until 1865 with the support of the powerful Catholic church.

1871 saw a sort of Liberal Revolution, led by Junto Rufino Barrios. He attempted to modernize the country by improving trade, building factories, introducing new crops. Coffee became an important product and attracted investment from outside the country, particularly from Germany. Barrios attacked the powerful church and instituted a constitution. He even had hopes of reuniting Central America and when he was thwarted by lack of cooperation from the other governments, took the country to war. There he died on the battlefield in 1885. For a few years, short-term leaders tried to solidify Rufino's reforms but when Jose Maria Barrios was assassinated in 1898 by a Swiss national, a true tyrant took control and ruled by force for 22 years.

It is said that when the chamber met after Barrios' assassination to select a leader, Manuel Estrada Cabrera, who had not been invited, strode in with his revolver, placed it on the table and said,

Gentlemen, you are looking at the president of Guatemala.

He remained in power for more than 20 years through use of the tried and true instruments of terror - manipulation of the political parties, an elaborate spy system, intimidation, armed police, mysterious murders, arbitrary imprisonments and executions. Laws prohibited the importation of weapons and arms and the people felt defenseless and helpless. Cabrera had no personal popularity but there was neither the spirit nor the will to rebel. It was during this period that the United Fruit Company got its stronghold in Guatemala. In exchange for agreeing to finish building the railroad from Guatemala City to the Atlantic port of Puerto Barrios,

Cabrera granted the UFC 170,000 acres of land on the Atlantic coast. By 1930, it was the largest employer and exporter in Guatemala. But the country was chosen not alone for its prime banana land but because it had the most corrupt and pliable government in the area.

Cabrera was in power until 1920. Franc and Will undoubtedly met him in the course of Will's diplomatic duties as vice consul at Livingston. Among Franc's memorabilia is the president's card. Franc wrote little about Cabrera himself but the corruption and bureaucratic dysfunction she encountered after Will's death in trying to get her property rights or any sort of official assistance, was a situation that started at the top.

Early Days

What we know about Will and Franc's earliest days in Guatemala comes from letters Franc wrote to friends. In November, 1888, she wrote to the Susans about her new life:

> *I have been existing all over the place. We have not spent more than 1 or 2 consecutive days in any one spot. We have no home. We have a roof in several places but we are leading a nomadic life. When we move on, we take a couple of changes in case of wetting which we often get, a few toilet articles and our bed which consists of a mosquito bar and mat....*

She went on to describe a rafting accident where they lost some of their possessions, including her class ring, and noted,

> *I am gradually severing my connections with civilization and drifting into barbarism.*

On the other hand, she had been several times to Puerto Barrios and gone dancing. She said that Will played the piano at the big hotel there and since she was often the only woman, she was passed from one man to the other without missing a step - often until broad daylight.

Ending that letter, Franc said:

It is so much trouble and expense to get anything pertaining to civilization as everything comes from the States...that I long ago made up my mind to live as near like the natives as I could accustom myself to. It is far the best way and I am not tied down to any one place and am at liberty to go anywhere with my husband.

But, as we shall see, they did finally settle at their San Francisco *finca* and, though often on the move, made it their jungle home.

Chapter 6
MAHOGANYLAND

Beginning in January of 1900, we have 25 years of diaries in which Franc recorded the day by day activities of her life. The diaries she kept in Guatemala up until Will's death in 1909 were large ledger-size books called Letts's Indian and Colonial Rough Diary - or sometimes Scribbling Diary. They seem to have been published with the employees of the British colonial service in mind and contain useful information about exchange rates, tide tables, calendars (including Jewish and Mohammedan), names of British consuls and other civil servants in the various outposts of the globe. There were advertisements for products that would be useful for residents both at home and abroad and included everything from bird seeds to iron staircases to scotch whiskey distillers. One visualizes busy civil servants from Delhi to Dublin perusing similar pages, making their notes and browsing the offerings that would - perhaps - make their lives more comfortable.

Each diary page was divided into three days of notes and each page was followed by a blotting sheet, necessary to absorb the flowing ink of that time. Some days Franc wrote nothing or perhaps just a sentence or two. Some days there was much to write and her notes extended around the margins. On most days she recorded the temperature and weather conditions such as rain or dry spells. In the diaries she kept from 1900-1905, most of the entries relate to their business of harvesting mahogany and include very little personal material. She wrote about their co-workers - foremen at the various camps, ship captains, laborers, cattle drivers and trainmen and gave details of the money or equipment given to company employees who were under their supervision. Included were oil, guns, cots, utensils for eating and cooking, machetes, food, sheep dip, coffee, nails, hay, moccasins, chains.

Harvesting mahogany was a labor intensive operation. It required the hiring of hundreds of workers and housing and provisioning them for the season - about 10 months at a time. It required several head of cattle to pull the trucks that would haul the wood out once it was cut.

The hiring began around Christmas time and involved a trip by Will and Franc to Belize where they could find Hondurans who, Franc noted, were larger and stronger and more suited to the work with lumber than the Mayan Indians and Caribs in the vicinity of the Rio Dulce. They would hire about 100 men for the season and each man would contract for a specific amount of work. If he did not complete the work he had promised, the worker was to come back the next year and finish it. Many of the men brought families with them and they made their homes in huts near the mahogany camps. They also brought their dogs, their turkeys and chickens, their pet parrots and various members of the monkey family. It took on the appearance of a settlement.

The settlement had to fed and otherwise provisioned. The lumber company was responsible for this and one of the Browns' jobs as manager was to assure that what was needed was available. It was a continual struggle. Provisions arrived by train and there were innumerable hang-ups - flooded tracks, delays at the port, broken down engines. If there was no food, the men walked off the job and police had to bring them back. Along with food, they needed hammocks, lantern wicks, chains for the cattle, ammonia, epsom salts, cigars, items of clothing - all the necessities (and a few amenities - there were always cigars and rum) for several hundred people to live for nine months in the midst of the jungle.

One of the first tasks when they arrived in February of 1900 was building houses for themselves and the other managers or section bosses. Names mentioned as working in the camps that year include Don Marco, Captain D, Graham, Captain Potts, and Jekyll. Fred Jekyll was destined to be a part of Franc's life for the next 12 years. When the mahogany business ended, around 1907, Jekyll and Brown became partners in a banana plantation. After Will's death, Jekyll and Franc were the co-owners and conflicts over their claims to the business made them bitter enemies. But until then, he was a constant in their lives. Like many of their other friends in Guatemala, Jekyll was of German ancestry, the Germans having settled there years before in the region of Coban where they developed the coffee industry.

Along with building their houses, one of their first jobs was to build a corral for the cattle. The jungle was seething with predatory intruders and the livestock had to be protected from all manner of dangerous creatures. It was necessary to be armed and ready. Franc, in her years there, became an excellent shot and always carried a revolver in case of emergences. She also went hunting, on occasion, and was adept with a Winchester rifle. In her writings years later, she enjoyed referring to herself as a "slender girl" - but she seems to have been a bit more of an Annie Oakley.

How did they do it?

Franc wrote an article about the business of harvesting mahogany which was published in *The Tropic Magazine.* It is worth summarizing here, to understand this process that recurred every year for the six they remained in the jungle - locating the trees to be cut, getting to them, felling them, and finally, getting them to the port. Each man had his job and was unlikely to deviate from it. Once a location was found where there seemed to be sufficient timber, the *hunters* were sent on ahead to find camp sites near good water. The next task was to cut a sort of road, called a "truck pass" which could accommodate a "creole truck" that was used to haul out the wood. This contraption was large and clumsy, having solid wooden wheels and requiring two to three yoke of oxen to pull it empty, and 5 or 6 when a log was on it.

The truck passes went from the railroad or river bank to the center of the main batch of wood, then smaller roads or *picetes* were cut to get to the individual trees. At the entrance to these smaller roads, there would be a palm leaf stuck and the number of knots in it indicated the number of trees to be cut on that road. The *fellers* - 2 men to a tree - would go to the tree they were to fell and clear the area around it. Then, when necessary, they would build a scaffolding of poles and vines so they could get above the huge spurs that some trees had. They would then take up their saws and work away until the giant was ready to fall.

Franc was fascinated and in awe of that moment when the tree toppled and wrote about it several times.

> *The moment is indicated by the creaking sounds of the breaking of the uncut portion of the tree. You begin to hold your breath, then to quiver and vibrations are produced in your whole being which affect seemingly your soul as well as your body; as the tree gets underway on its downgrade, the spell is broken and you scamper away to a safer distance, as the final vast reverberation sounds and resounds through the boundless jungle. It can be heard for miles and miles around as the giant carries many of its companions with it as it falls, being bound strongly to them by huge, tough vines.*

In a different article, she wrote even more dramatically.

> *Interminably, it would seem, straight from the fresh-cut bleeding stretches a huge mahogany form. Its topmost branches are lying prone, so far distant that the natives, sweating and triumphant, must needs use their machetes to cut a new path to find them and in its downward plunge, the tree has smashed smaller brothers, snapping them as if they were match sticks.*

When the fallen tree was cleared of underbrush, the *junkers* went in to do their work which was to cut it into manageable lengths - 12, 15 or 20 feet. The *liners* then came along and the logs were lined up for the *rough beaters*. Two sides were beaten and the log was turned over. The *fellers* then came back to work. 6 or 8 of them lined up beside the log with poles which were used to turn the log over. They shoved their pointed poles as far as possible under the log, the other end of it on their right shoulder. A "chanty man" began to sing and when he got to "Turn-the-log-ove-ver," they all lifted. Then half held while the other half shoved the pole under again - then the chanting began again; this went on until the log was over.

The last step in preparation for getting the logs out of the jungle was squaring them off. The *broad axe* men did this, smoothing the log off until the two opposite sides are the exact same measurement and as perfect as if having gone through a sawmill. Not a particle of bark was to be left.

When all this was accomplished, the log was ready to be hauled to the railroad or river - the embarcadero. The passes were often very muddy and the crude and heavy creole truck could not get through. In those cases, the logs were placed on rough-hewn sleds or dragged long with chains. Franc also described another conveyance, the Deckerville track, which involved two little trucks. One end of the log was placed on one truck and the other end on another; she wrote that she liked to perch on top of the log and have a ride with..

...all the glee and excitement of a child.

When the logs arrived at the railroad they could be loaded onto flatbed cars and transported to the port.

Mahogany logs on the Motagua River

But an easier and less expensive way of getting the wood out was to use the rivers and streams entirely. If the available water was a broad, slow-flowing stream, the logs were bound together with chains and poles so that a firm, floor-like surface was made. The workers would make their camps on these big rafts along with families, dogs and fowls and float placidly down to the sea. On the other hand, if the stream was more turbulent, narrower, the rafts must be more pliable so there is less danger of coming apart in whirlpools or when striking drift wood or a tree. The rafts could be torn apart. Only agile, brave swimmers were placed on those rafts and they were followed by crews in *pitpains* who could rescue them when necessary.

The first year

On January 8, 1900, the workers had been hired in Belize - and Franc celebrated her 31st birthday. She wrote that she was not going to tell her age any more. Will's gift to her was 30 gold pieces and another gift came in news from home that her sister Bess had just had a baby girl whom she had named Gladys.

Two weeks later, they were home at San Francisco *finca* and expecting a visit from A. Arathoon who seems to have been the main representative in the area for the Chambers Guthrie company. When he arrived, he was ill for a few days and in February, Franc noted that they had gotten a "hard letter" from him after he left. She did not explain the problem but answered it at once.

The house at San Francisco *finca*

Franc began to mention the workers who seemed to be about the house frequently. Brown was a cook who was there when she arrived and she decided to keep him until she was more settled. Lindo and Pedro were engaged in building the corral for cattle and also working on the houses for Don Marco and other overseers. People were in and out constantly - Pitts, Don Marco, Dandy, Jekyll and others who seemed to be section bosses, as well as the company bookkeeper who paid frequent visits.

Franc wrote to the Susans that they had three camps under their special charge with three others to look after in a general way so they were busy all the time. At the *finca*, she was doing some "farming" - planting flowers and trying to raise chickens - with which, she noted, she didn't have much luck. There were a number of animals on the place and she and Will found them entertaining - since, after all, what else was there? One of the Susans had said that Franc had an "ideal life." So now, Franc wrote, whenever anything went wrong, she and Will would laugh and remind themselves that they did.

In many ways, it really is and I am pretty sure I never could be content to live very far away from the ideal part of this life. It unfits one for any other life.

On March 16, Franc mentioned a guest who would become a lifelong friend. George Byron Gordon was an archaeologist who arrived by train to study the nearby Mayan ruins at Quirigua. Later he became well known for establishing the department of archaeology at the University of Pennsylvania and their world famous archaeology museum. The Brown home was a hospitable one and he returned there off and on for the next couple of years.

The mahogany work progressed. On the 19th, Will bought $20 worth of rum to celebrate the first logs that were felled. The two creole trucks that would help get them out were finished and were given names, "Break of Day" and "Never Delay." Then came a significant break in the arrival of food and other provisions with the result that men walked off the job. Will went to Puerto Barrios and gathered some soldiers to help bring them back. Some were tracked down in Livingston. Several had found work unloading boats and were reluctant to return to the jungle until that was finished. It was mid-April before they got most of them back. By that time, Pitts and his crew had cut some beautiful wood, including a huge log that took a week to get out of the forest.

By May 17, there were 108 logs in the river, ready to float down to the port. There was much difficulty in getting another very large log out and the steamer that was waiting at Port was threatening to leave without it. By the time it was finally loaded on June 21, a month had passed.

In July and August, the rains came in torrents and rivers were high. A bridge was washed out at Amates as were several miles of train track. Franc referred to this period as the "heaviest floods known around here." Two men who were working with the cattle were caught up in a palm tree and unable to get down for two days. Fences were washed away. At one point, in August, the train did not come for a week. There were logs still to be loaded. It was all was going far too slowly.

During this period in 1900, Franc mentioned several times that she suffered from chills and fever and saw a doctor in Livingston who prescribed quinine and calomel. The spell of fever she had described in Mexico may have been the onset of the malaria from which she suffered periodically during her years in Guatemala and for some time beyond. She noted in a letter to the Susans:

> *I am beginning to fear the climate is getting the better of me. I am losing flesh all the time and my hair is coming out by the handsful.*

Franc rarely used the word malaria for her spells of fever but she soon became something of an expert at treating it in other expatriates, almost all of whom were afflicted at some point. But she also wrote during this period that she had learned to swim, float, dive and..

> *..do any old thing in the water except go to the bottom.*

In October, they were coming to the end of the harvesting seasoning and winding down the operation. Franc ordered rope and chains to prepare for building a raft to get the final logs down the rivers. By the end of October, 22 lots were hauled out and rafted with 34 lots that were already on the river. They began rounding up cattle from the camps and sending them down by train; settling with the men; and packing up their things to be ready to leave the *finca* for their winter visit to Belize.

In November, there was another visit from Gordon who was photographing at Quirigua. As the work wound down, Franc had time to go fishing but then had another bout of fever. She remarked on November 2 that McKinley was elected president of the U.S. and that they were loading the last of the wood.

On December 4, they finally left for Port and, on the 13th, left there for Belize. There they had a session or two with lawyers - probably in connection with the men who had walked off the job in March - but all issues were resolved. They began at once to hire men for the coming year and had signed on 100 by Christmas Eve when they watched boat races on the river. But Will was not well for most of that week and on New Year's Eve, Franc went to church alone.

So ended their first year in Mahoganyland. There would be six more before they ended their association with Chambers, Guthrie and Company. All would follow a similar work schedule - but the only certainty in their lives was that there would be uncertainty. Along with the natural disasters of floods and torrential rains, they would encounter an infinite variety of human foibles.

Chapter 7
SETTLING IN

The diary that Franc kept in 1901 - the second year of the mahogany work - was the most complete of any she kept while in Guatemala. She wrote almost every day and included details about workers, what she paid them, what they did or didn't do, the number of cattle being rounded up, the logs harvested, the provisions distributed. At the back of this diary there is a record of all financial transactions - wages paid out to workers by name and what she paid for items bought, everything from moccasins to sugar. She also included a page called "One Day's Occupation," dated September 25, 1901, an account of how she spent a typical day in the jungles. Overall, her life followed a pattern similar to that of 1900.

There was the hiring of the workers in Belize, the innumerable difficulties of provisioning them, the fights among them, their tendency to walk off the job at the slightest provocation, the physical injuries, the attacks of malaria, and the missing cattle which had to be found.

But early 1901 did bring a respite for Will and Franc in the form of a vacation - a trip to the States to visit Franc's family for the first time since heading south in 1896. Having completed hiring workers in Belize in early January, Franc and Will, along with Arathoon and Graham, left for Puerto Barrios. They spent a couple of days making arrangements to get the workers up to the camps. Then the Browns were ready to leave. Franc wrote on January 10:

> *This day we celebrate after 4 long years in the tropics. We set sail this morning for New Orleans on the mail boat "Still Water."*

Three days later they disembarked and began their month-long visit to friends and family in the States.

The trip seems to have been something of a disappointment. In New Orleans, they stayed at the new St. Charles hotel and embarked on a round of shopping. But within the week, Franc got a cold and remained unwell for most of the remainder of their visit in the States. Perhaps it was the change in climate. But after two weeks in New Orleans, she left for Dyersburg, TN, where Bess lived, still feeling ill. While there, she was treated by a doctor for...

..rhinogitis, farengitis, bronchitis, tonsillitis and laryngitis (!)

Franc seemed to feel that the family was not exactly killing the fatted calf for her. In Dyersburg, she noted that she found them all asleep and more or less ill. After a week there she felt somewhat better and left for Cairo, IL, to visit her sister Sallie's family, the Pennebakers. There, she wrote that..

...no one met us and no one was home when we got there.

But they stayed for a week and both she and Will spent some time in the dentist's chair, catching up with all the fillings and extractions required after four years in the jungle. They visited other family members in Columbus, Kentucky, and then returned to New Orleans where they sailed on February 21 for Guatemala and their jungle home.

In early March they were back at the *finca* and ready to oversee the wood cutting. Franc immediately began to organize the work around the house and requisition supplies for the camps. When she wrote in her diary in September of that year an account of a typical day in her life, she must have chosen one of the quieter ones. It sounds rather like that of a busy housewife and could almost have been happening on a farm anywhere in the States in 1901.

As soon as I was out of bed, went through some swaboda (?) exercises. Then dressed, at the same time tidied the room and drank a cup of tea. Had breakfast, made a collar for 'baby' (a pet?) - by putting a buckle on a piece of belt. Put pillows, night clothes, towels out to sun, etc.

Darned a long place in a pajama coat, darned some holes in a pair of drawers and sewed the covers of a silk hndkf (?) Brushed and folded a coat and put away. Made some liquid camphor by putting gum camphor in alcohol, rubbed my face and neck good with the alcohol. Put gum camphor in chests and on all shelves.

Made a dozen bandages by tearing an old night dress into strips and sewing 2 pieces together to make them long enough and rolling each one ready for use. In the mean time, read a business letter my husband had just written, as is my custom, believing as we do that two heads are better than one. Suggested some additions he had not thought of. Also, I put down my work, went to the kitchen and got some pepper and gave it to a little native girl who had been sent by her mother to ask for it, as my boy was scrubbing the verandas. Then we had lunch. After lunch, I finished the bandages and put them away and then took a long siesta. I then went out to perform an operation on one of our dog's tail, it having been chopped off when hunting. While I was away in the back yard making ready, I came in to give some medicine to a man who had come complaining of aching teeth and gums. Then we amputated the tail well above the old wound, bound it tight to stop the bleeding, then gave him a thorough scrubbing with hot water, soap and scrubbing brush. Then rubbed on a mixture of lard and suet for mange, then dressed his tail properly.

I came in and changed my clothes throughout - which is not a very lengthy procedure, being in the tropics and a hot day. Then I sat down for some more sewing, putting fresh embroidery around the neck of a wipili. Then we put on bathing clothes and walked a mile to the river for a swim. Then strolled back again, changed clothes and sat down for a few seconds rest before dinner. After dinner, at 7 I went out and re-dressed the tail as it was bleeding badly. I forgot to mention dressing the hand of a boy, the palm of which had been cut wide open about a week ago. And which I had been attending to ever since. Then I attempted a little reading, fighting the mosquitoes all the time.

Of course, through the day, I directed all the work of the house, kitchen and garden.

But this description doesn't fully convey the constant activity, the comings and goings of workers, arrivals and departures of the section bosses, conflicting messages from Chambers, Guthrie. In April, the *alcalde* arrived with orders to stop work at all the camps. However, this was reversed when they heard from Arathoon and they continued with the cutting.

In April, archaeologist George Gordon was back in Quirigua and Franc was packed and ready to go there when she began to have fever again. Chico was sent by mule to get a doctor to come and see her and after several days, he did. On Apr 22, Gordon arrived at their *finca* by private rail car with a beautiful *wipili* for Franc and remained a week. Then Franc and Will joined his party in returning to Quirigua where they stayed for a few days.

Quirigua is a Mayan ruin, considerably smaller than Tikal or even Copan in Honduras. It is located in the midst of a dense rainforest and, at that time, had been little visited compared to other more famous Mayan sites. The United Fruit Company bought the site later, in 1909, along with vast acres of land on which they planted bananas. Though under different ownership, these plantations now stretch to the horizon in all directions.

Quirigua history dates from about 300 BC when migrants from the Yucatan established themselves as rulers and it was a place of power and prosperity until the 8th century AD. The *stelae* at the ruins are the tallest in the Mayan world and the site includes some bizarre *zoomorphs* - six blocks of stone carved with interlacing animal and human figures. A few Europeans visited it as early as 1840 and, in 1881, archaeologist Alfred Maudsley paid several visits, taking photographs and making plaster molds of inscriptions. In the 1970's, the University of Pennsylvania and National Geographic did extensive work at the site and in 1981, it was designated as a UNESCO World Heritage site.

Franc seems to have first visited Quirigua on a hunting expedition with the local head hunter. Her description was:

> *They are located about 60 miles from Puerto Barrios up the Guatemala Northern Railway and some 3 miles into the jungle from the road bed. They consist of impressive pillars or monuments, varying in height from fifteen to seventy feet. In general form, they arrange themselves into a quadrangle or ampitheater. Dotted here*

and there, through the swamp and bogs and dense undergrowth
rise huge mounds of stone, turtle-like, frog-like, or taking the shape
of weird gray globes festooned with ferns and creepers. These are
scarred with surface hieroglyphics, figures and emblems.

Gordon had gone to Honduras to work at the Copan site along with
other archaeologists but in March of 1900, political upheavals there had
made it expedient for them to leave the country. Quirigua was nearby
and largely unexplored so rather than hurrying back to the states,
Gordon headed there, taking the train that passed the Brown *finca*. As
noted earlier, they welcomed him, wined and dined him and began a
friendship that lasted throughout their lives.

Franc being Guatemalan

Gordon returned to visit more than once that spring, bringing gifts -
photos, mineral water, tins of flour, and another lovely *wipili* for Franc.
He had made molds of the Quirigua ruins and when he was ready to
take them back to the states, one of the carpenters who worked for
Will and Frank made boxes for them and helped load them on the

train. When he left the area, he gave Will his two saddles and a case of mineral water.

He was gone my mid-May and life returned to normal - normal being trips up and down the line, checking in at the camps, moving the cattle around as needed, seeing that food for workers and animals was available, caring for the sick or wounded. There were breaks for Will and Franc off and on when they went to Livingston to shop and have a taste of what passed for "civilization."

But back in the jungle, work was not going well. Among other things, there was a pitched battle between two of the camps' section gangs. Machetes and guns were involved but no one was hurt - except for

...one fat woman who was sent to her house and spanked.

In June there were heavy rains and the track was washed out. There were injuries among the men - one came in with a bad hand, having smashed it between two logs. One worker was met out on the road with his woman, her hands tied together as he dragged her along, with a revolver in the other hand.

As July came, there was still wood to get out and they decided to try to send it to the port by train rather than by water - but the train, of course, was anything but reliable. Sometimes if the train did not come, Franc and Will rode a pushcar to get to the camps; this was a small open car that could be propelled along the train tracks by pumping a handle. Their house workers - Nicassio, Chico, Lindo, and Tusio - were alternately helpful and temperamental, getting angry when corrected and refusing to work.

In a July entry, Franc first used the code she developed when she wanted to keep an entry secret. It involved substituting symbols and reversed letters for the letters of the alphabet and, while not very difficult to crack, is enough to slow one down in reading. She seemed to use it primarily when talking about Will's drinking and sometimes her own. She also used it when talking about her own health problems or her romantic relationships with men, both before and after Will's death.

At this point, however, in 1901, she just mentioned in code "Mr. B stopped whisky." Though this is her first mention of his inclination to drink heavily, it suggests that he was already inclined to "overdo" it - something that increased as the years passed.

As noted, work in the mahogany forests followed a pattern each year: hire workers in Belize in January, set up camps, find trees to cut down, mark them, cut and square them off, haul them to the port. But in July of 1901, they were still in need of hunters - those who would find the trees to cut - and looked for them at Morales, Andes and Amates. Some men were discharged, others got busy rounding up cattle. New trees were found but there was continued flooding to interfere with the cutting.

They struggled constantly with the lack of provisions. Franc's explanation was that often this was due to..

> *..violent demonstrations of the great forces of nature - disastrous hurricanes, devastating floods, destructive earthquakes and other acts of God.*

There was much grumbling by the workers about being given plantain as ration. The result was that some men walked off the job and in mid-August, Franc and Will had to make a trip to Belize to deal with the situation. Will was summoned to appear in court on September 2. While there, they saw friends and went to church and called at the governor's house. Eventually, Arathoon arrived and the case was decided in the company's favor with a settlement of $10 each given by the men. Franc noted that it was..

> *..a great gain for labor hirers in or out of colony.*

Remote from the world as they often felt, Franc kept up with outside events and noted that on September 6, the president of the U.S. was shot in Buffalo and that, on the 14th, McKinley died.

They returned to the mahogany camp by the end of September and spent the remaining months of 1901 winding up the cutting and hoping that they would be continuing for another year. They found that some of the cattle and oxen had gotten away due to the carelessness of Tusio and Chiquito so they were told to find them and that there would be no more pay until they did.

As the summer wound down, they were promised by the railroad officials that they could begin loading the logs onto the train "any day now." At the same time, at Morales, wood was being rafted down to the port. Cattle were being rounded up and, through November, they continued to load in spite of never-ending labor problems. Chico and Pacheca would not work together; Tusio and Hernandez were still "at it". They received word from one of the bosses, Capt. Graham, that his men would not go down the river but when Will went to investigate, they denied that they were refusing to go and the work proceeded.

Finally, by Thanksgiving, the wood was out of the creek, the cattle rounded up, the laborers paid off, and supplies stored. A wire from Arathoon informed them that they could hire labor in Belize for one more year, at least. So, with this assurance of continued work, they enjoyed their end of year respite there, going to church, going to the Belize Cub, dancing. A British gunboat was in and officers added excitement to the social events. Franc, for all her self-proclaimed tendency to be "9/10 primitive," greatly enjoyed social events, dressing up and meeting sophisticated people.

Franc wrote the Susans that they always had a jolly time in Belize and that there was always a "wee bit" of betting going on. But between small limit poker, church raffles, etc., they came out about even at the end of the season. She wondered if her friends would find that "very shocking."

> *There are absolutely no pastimes here and one has to resort to such ways and means - which I think is quite harmless considering all things.*

There were also dances, lunches, teas, driving, riding, calls and receiving callers.

> *It is a queer shallow life and 3 weeks is quite sufficient for me - and 4 weeks is almost unbearable.*

Chapter 8
TRAVELING AND DINING OUT

After Will died in 1910 and Franc returned to the U.S. with not much money and her living to make, she wrote stories of her Guatemalan experiences, hoping to get paid for them. With a few, she succeeded and they were printed in magazines and newpapers. Others remained unpublished. But the manuscripts are lively and informative and often more fun to read than the diary entries. While the diaries are full of day-to-day details about plantation business, the manuscripts are more emotional and embellished with opinions, flights of fancy, and dramatic descriptions. They covered a variety of topics - rafting in flooded streams, setting up her own private zoo, hunting jaguars at Quiriqua, fishing in alligator infested rivers, traveling in a variety of rail cars, visiting churches in Guatemala City and Antigua, and descriptions of the many possibilities for dining when provisions did not arrive. Looking at some of these will give us a livelier picture of life in Mahoganyland.

Pitpains **in Livingston harbor**

As we have seen, the Browns were on the go a great deal. But how they got from place to place depended on the part of the country they were in. Traveling by boat was necessary and frequent. When one arrived in

55

Puerto Barrios from Guatemala City or from any foreign port either in the US or abroad, there was no way to get from there to Livingston and the Rio Dulce except by water. Franc wrote:

> *The boats plying these waters are of the worst kind and would not be permitted to run in any waters in any other country...on one occasion, we were going over in a miserable little open flat bottom stern wheeler and when we neared Livingston, night came down and a heavy sea came up suddenly ...and as the big waves would strike we would have to seize anything available and hang on for dear life. ....When we were still some distance from the wharf, our fears were again aroused when we discovered there was not a light on board to signal ashore for assistance for there are some bad rocks near the mouth of the river towards which we seemed to be drifting and to add to our disagreeable sensations, we learned there was no such thing as an anchor on board to arrest our progress toward a possible wreck. One of the chief dangers of being overboard is the presence of innumerable sharks which infest those tropical waters. However, some man had a revolver which was immediately utilized for signaling.... small dories came out and took us to shore on the installment plan.*

This experience could have happened to anyone attempting to visit this Caribbean area of Guatemala, crossing from Puerto Barrios to Livingston. But Franc's experience rafting with the logs in the Montagua river was her choice, based on her determination to be involved in the mahogany business first hand. After all, she might have stayed back at the *finca* and left it all to Will. But that was never Franc's style. She wrote:

> *We were freeing a log right in the deepest water and strongest current when our pitpain got crossways of the current and was filled with water before we knew anything was wrong. Out we went, bag and baggage. I could not swim at the time so you can imagine my sensations. Howsomever we were not yet forgotten by our guardian angel and we soon scrambled to a place of safety on the log we were after and the men grabbed the raft before it was swept away and quickly had it bailed out. We once more embarked and continued*

to the little town nearby where we always spent out first night .... Everything we had on was soaked through and through so we had to remain until the sun came out the next day and dried us as we continued our journey down the treacherous river.

Another frequent mode of travel was on the back of a mule. Franc wrote that that held less danger than any other method. She wrote of a twenty-five mile trip over two high mountains where she had a splendid view of Lake Izabal. She insisted that they were perfectly safe riding a mule even at night and in a terrific storm. Another such trip was to coffee haciendas, winding up and up and up - to a distance of some five thousand feet and scenery that was worth the trip.

The train, however, was the most frequent method of travel from their jungle home. Franc wrote:

.. the Ferro carril del Norte de Guatemala holds the record for variety in the art of travel and is fraught with all the excitement and dangers the most venturesome could desire. We have traveled on the 'cow catcher,' in the engine, in the tender, in flat cars, in box cars, first and second class coaches and last but not least, 'No.5" the superintendent's private coach.

Due to the frequent floods, bridges were washed out from time to time and trains were a very uncertain quantity.

Once, in a fit of desperation for something to do for amusement, I took a notion that a moonlight trip to the port on a push car would be rather jolly. My husband was willing and we got the car and four men with long poles to push us along.

When they got to section 9 camp, they persuaded the adults there to let their 2 "young ladies" join them. (Franc did not name them so we are not sure who they were.) By that time they was a party of 8. It was hard work for the men to shove the car along over rails that were mostly out of sight, being covered with grass in many places. And it began to rain. Finally, when they got to the big hill, about ten miles from the port, they all had to walk while the men pushed the car up. The idea then was to get on it and coast down the two miles to the port. To get it to the top,

>...*the men would give the car a shove and overtake it and give another - but alas, alack, they gave it one push too many and down it went all by its lonesome.*

The ladies were left to enjoy their walk down the hill in the moonlight. They spotted some maiden hair fern in a rock cut and stopped to gather it - though it was the middle of the night. Meanwhile, at Section 2, the section boss spotted the runaway car and managed to stop it. So the ladies were able to ride the remaining distance to port, a wet and bedraggled group.

The trains ran erratically, due to the weather, to track problems and any number of other delays so when one arrived, Franc was likely to take it no matter how she had to ride. If there was no room in the box car, she might perch on the flat car, sitting on anything she could find handy. One day, the second class car was so crowded the conductor suggested some of them might have to sit in the box car which, he said, had only a few head of stock in it. They managed to avoid that experience but on the way back, two immense hogs were put right in with the passengers. Franc remarked that she was the only white woman who traveled regularly on that line and most of the passengers were natives, principally men. She wrote:

>*The bottle is ever present among them and every few minutes it is passed around and everyone has a drink of white-eye, an evil concoction of native rum with a vile smell.*

>*It is not uncommon to see two or three measuring their length on the filthy floor and sometimes dead to the world and foaming at the mouth from too much booze. No one pays any attention to them and when they reach their destination, some kind friend picks them up bodily and dumps them out on the platform.*

>*It might be more agreeable to ride with our "dumb creatures" as fellow passengers, after all.*

Dining

With this uncertainty about travel, supplies would not always arrive on time. Floods, hurricanes, violent rainstorms and even earthquakes plagued - and still plague - that part of the world. So sometimes the train tracks and bridges were out for days at a time. In that case, it could be a challenge to put together a meal. But Franc notes in one of her articles that, unlike Mother Hubbard, Mother Nature's cupboard is never bare. She went on to describe some of the possibilities to be found nearby.

There was the seed of a certain palm, deep yellow in color, which when boiled for a time, tastes just like turkey soup. There were mollusks (periwinkles) which could be gathered by the handfuls and, after soaking for a couple of days to get clean, were cooked with cornmeal dough and sucked out of the shell - delicious! Conch was a delicacy, though it had to be retrieved from the bottom of the sea by a diver. Turtles were found in abundance and the meat was fried - though it rather eerily continued to jump around for awhile in the pan.

Iguanas were delicious to eat and were considered a great delicacy in Belize. Franc insisted that when fried, the meat tasted exactly like fried chicken. And there were partridges which were almost all breast, along with pheasants, wild duck and parrot.

Eggs from iguanas and alligators were, according to Franc, quite delicious when scrambled with butter. They were almost entirely yoke. To go with the protein in this jungle feast, there was the heart of the cohun palm which tasted like cabbage, the fronds of the panama hat palm which were much like asparagus, and the yampa - like a sweet potato though purple in color. Tomatoes grew on vines and were used in almost every meal. Some flowers were eaten, too, and gave color to food, which the natives always loved.

Fruits were plums, monkey apples and cheeries. Tea could be made from the leaves of a huge jungle vine and from lemon grass. Chocolate was made from cocoa beans and an extract was made from vanilla beans. And to liven it all up, there was palm wine. A native would climb the tree and tap it near the top. A liquid was exuded and, when left to ferment, became an "oh be joyful" beverage.

In conclusion, Franc noted:

> *You can survive a long time if you know the secrets of the jungle.*

Chapter 9
HER JUNGLE ZOO

Franc loved animals. It is not surprising that she turned to them for companionship and as compensation in a life that could have been crushingly lonely. Will was frequently away at the camps supervising the mahogany work and she was left for days at a time with only the native servants for company. So she made friends with the jungle creatures that surrounded her and welcomed them to her compound. And the first inhabitant of her little zoo was not a mild-mannered, easily tamed monkey but a tiger cat!

One morning Franc heard a knock at the door of her Big House on the *finca*. It was Lindo, a Ladino chief whose wife Franc had cured of a fever. He called to pay his respects and thank her and to bring a present - a baby tiger, as soft and fluffy as a kitten. She couldn't refuse but took him in and fed him from a bottle until his legs were strong and he could move around. Of course, he soon became a rather formidable creature with glistening teeth and the blood of the wild in his veins. So a cage was built for him to the rear of the *finca* where he would lie for hours gazing out towards the jungle.

The tiger was the beginning of Franc's plantation zoo which eventually contained baboons, spider monkeys, ant-eaters, raccoons, hunting dogs, deer, a variety of birds. The natives came to look upon animal-giving as a fad where Franc was concerned. They called her "the Patrona" and would rarely approach the San Francisco *finca* without a living gift in tow. A tract was cleared back of the Big House and a corral fence built around it to keep out jungle prowlers. Lindo and the native boys built cages of wire and wood for those creatures which needed to be contained.

Infant baboons were brought and fed by bottle, becoming quickly domesticated. Night walkers arrived from the Quiriqua ruins and turned out to be great playmates for the plantation puppies. One of their tricks was to wrap their long tales around a puppy's neck and drag him about the yard as he barked in protest. The spider monkeys played a bit rough, scampering up the tall palm trees and throwing nuts at the other members of the zoo. An anteater was not a particularly chummy personality around the finca but demanded attention from Franc - he would follow her around begging for milk which she fed him with an eye dropper. He became quite friendly with some of the night walkers and they would hang out together under the trees foraging for insects.

There were a number of dogs on the finca but Lindo was the one who brought the two favorite hunting dogs - John Bull and Uncle Sam. It seemed that no one in Guatemala went anywhere without a hunting dog. These two, like most, were not pure bred but a combination of almost everything and able to withstand the country's hardships, such as the vicious insects of the long rainy season, including prodigious swarms of mosquitoes.

But the favorite zoo inhabitants seemed to be two deer - Baby and Charlie. They were brought to Franc as babies by one of the native chiefs as pay for quinine which he needed. As the deer grew, they were granted privileges unknown to the other animals and wandered freely through the house - through the dining room at mealtimes, or lying next to Franc in bed when she was ill with a spell of malaria. They joined her on a hunting trip with Lindo and the pack of hunting dogs, including John Bull and Uncle Sam. The hunters were looking for meat to feed the dogs but were especially on the lookout for armadillo to add to the zoo. They managed to bring back five of them - one for the zoo and the others to be eaten, as they are a highly cherished white meat in that part of the world. On the same trip, they captured a peccary and a tapir to add to Franc's collection. All this was accomplished without firing a shot, although Franc had her trusty Winchester in hand.

The menagerie grew, with the addition of a wild hog who liked to sit in the Patrona's lap and a collection of birds - macaws, paroquettes, ten species of parrots and a toucan. These winged creatures filled wooden cages behind the big house and decorated the area with their dazzling yellow, red, green and blue plumage. There were also delicate miniature love birds in pairs, cooing and bill-kissing. Colorful macaws were there also but, if left uncaged, their sharp beaks could tear chunks from the furniture and buttons off all their clothes.

Just on the outskirts of the plantation, there were creeks and small lakes and ponds. Great flocks of ducks came to them - mallards, gadwell, canvasback, teal. There were also cranes and egrets and pelicans and gulls and pheasants. In writing about all these avian beauties, Franc did not forget the quetzal, that Guatemalan symbol found on money and coats of arms and on official insignia. She wrote that the male is a magnificient bird -a rich metallic green with flashes of vivid carmine on head and breast - though whether she ever had actually seen one in the vicinity of her plantation, we are not sure. Their habitat is the high mountains in the district where coffee was grown. But Franc added as she wrote this years later,

> *..above me, on a mahogany stand, there looks down on me with calm, cruel eyes, a mounted quetzal.*

Fishing

Franc, during her time in Guatemala was never far away from water. At the mahagony plantations she was near the Motagua River and several other rivers and streams. At Tameja, she lived on the banks of Tameja creek and was only a short distance from the Rio Dulce. So fishing was a part of daily life. She wrote that they almost always used only a line and hook and varied the bait according to the fish they were trying to catch. Some of them loved fruit, including overripe bananas. Sardines could be scooped up by the handfuls. A favorite sport was torch fishing when the boats rowed close to shore and men held up pine torches to attract the fish which came in droves and were harpooned.

Of course, in the process, Franc also encountered more dangerous creatures - such as sharks, alligators and crocodiles. She related her experience with an alligator who was eating the ducks from her pond. To catch him, she draped some meat over a limb near the water's edge. At the other end, she tied a tin filled with pebbles. In the night, there was a great rattling sound and she went out with her shotgun. She wrote:

> *Mr. Alligator, in these waters, never eats where he hunts. He*
> *must sneak quietly away with his prize to his mud dining room.*

There she found him and got him with an easy shot from her Winchester. She wrote that he was the largest specimen seen in the Rio Dulce - with 300 stones found in his stomach!

There were, of course, snakes in the area of her plantations, including a hideous Tommy Goff which Franc found coiled in a dresser drawer. This was not something she chose to add to her zoo. It was the most dreaded of the reptiles, being dark green in color, hard to spot in the jungle and having a venom that was almost medicine-proof. There were also green whip snakes that hung from tree branches and jauls that wrapped themselves around rodents and crushed them to death.

Surrounding this varied and abundant animal life was lush and even more abundant plant life. There was wild fig, many variety of palms, a lignum vitae that rivaled the lilac in tint and texture. Towering over all were cottonwoods as high as 70 feet. Mangroves lined the banks of streams and rivers. And there were ferns, begonias, air plants and an abundance of orchids. Franc wrote:

> *One must go to Guatemala to see orchids!*

Franc's love of all this natural beauty was genuine and carried with it a naturalist's curiosity and desire to understand her surroundings . But she was practical and knew that sometimes the birds and fish must be their food and that wild animals which threatened tamer creatures must be destroyed - so a hunting trip was never out of the question entirely.

Hunting

Though Franc preferred capturing to killing, she did enjoy hunting as a sport and wrote a lengthy description of a trip in the Quirigua ruins where she shot a puma, a jaguar and an ocelot. Natividad, the chief head-hunter of the jungles around the mahogany camps, came one day to tell her that there might be great sport for her if she would like to accompany them to Quirigua. It had been reported that calves were missing from the cattle herds nearby and a huge jaguar with bloody jowls had been spotted near the ruins. Of course, she wanted to go with them - nothing would make her happier! She wrote:

> *The head hunter was bronzed and graven idol hewn from the very forest of mahogany he knew so well. For Natividad was old past all reckoning....Once, while entering a virgin mahogany forest, he pointed up to one of the giants and said a bit sadly: "Me see when tree little baby - so high. Now look. Maybe me too be cut down by white man some day."*

> *....He knew the jungle and the jungle creatures as no other native could hope to know them. He sensed their subtleties and their problems. No question concerning these animals ever went unanswered and it was from him I gained my deep insight into the Quirigua ruins. This puma - this wild boar - this anteater - this sullen jaguar that came stealing at night across the jungle and stopped only at the portals of the Big House - he knew their water holes, their salt licks, their favorite food.....I have always considered it a high form of compliment that Natividad liked me - trusted me - wanted to be in the position of guarding me against dangers which my call of the wild encouraged.*

Franc was ready at dawn the next day. A party of mozoes had gone ahead to look out for difficult passages and prepare the trail. She mounted her mule, riding in a western saddle which, she insisted, was not really uncomfortable. They waded through an alligator-infested stream and through cesspools of jungle waste, the mule sometimes mired up to his belly. At one point, Natividad carried Franc across to the other shore. It took them 3 hours to cover 13 miles once they entered the swampy area.

Franc, of course, carried her regulation army rifle, a present from Will. He always enjoyed teasing her about her desire to join the hunt, calling her a "born savage." Cabrera's government at that time had placed a strict ban on rifles and they were seldom found in private hands. Will clearly had some sort of "in" with the powers that be in order to get one and also the ammunition for it. Franc never asked how Will had managed it but took very good care of it, keeping it oiled and cased.

The gun bearers also had weapons but they were shot- guns of ancient vintage, requiring ramrods and powder.

As they approached the ruins, Natividad spotted the tracks of wild boar and they followed them to a wallow of black muck where the animal had wandered.

> *This boar was a fine speciman. He stood erect in a shallow place for a single second and there was something almost statue-like in his pose. The muscular back and shoulder and the well-set lithe legs all indicated extreme agility. His ivory-like tusks - long, large, polished and curved upward - were as superb as any I had ever seen.*

The unlucky tusker was so engrossed in his mud bath, he never suspected that he had company. The first shot got him - it is unclear whether it was Franc who fired it but she went home with the tusks.

The hunting party continued to the ruins where they set up camp. This consisted of native-built shackalows made of poles with a roof of palms - an airy and durable hut. Franc wrote that she could not but enthuse over their hunting ground. There they were in a jungle as trackless as any, yet within touch of the mysterious remnants of a civilization that had hunted there centuries before. Franc walked away from the camp and climbed on top of the one of the slabs and there, having left her rifle against a stone, spotted a huge anteater having a dinner of honey and termites. She wrote:

> *I wanted to laugh as he waddled out for a moment into an open area. Was there ever a funnier gait? he is the most awkward animal of the jungle due, I think, to his inability to walk firmly on the cushions of his strong, stiff feet. The three claws of each foot are doubled under and the middle claw is quite long, curled and formidable....This speciman was larger than my own* (in her zoo) *and in wonderful condition....But the outcome of this was less sportsmanlike than I would have liked. A breeze caught my black tie and flaunted it. In an instant the animal was away, lumbering straight for the camp where the mozoes promptly killed it.*

However, Franc's desire to be sportsmanlike seems not to have applied to the animals they encountered later in the evening. Perhaps this is because they were predators which threatened the cattle herds - that, indeed, was the reason for the hunt. As Franc sat in the evening in a shelter near their bonfire, she saw two spots of phosphorescent light burning against the jungle wall. The gun bearer nearby nudged her. She knew that Natividad and others had seen what she had - but they wanted to give her the first chance. She knelt on the ground and took aim and fired. Other firearms sounded as well and the bag for the evening was far better than they had hoped. Franc had shot a large and beautiful puma. The others had gotten her mate and later in the night, an ocelot and another puma.

But Natividad was not happy - the jaguar was still at large and he was determined to find him.

Him big brute. We get him!

And they did. Natividad constructed a jaguar trap - a deep hole, eight feet square - covered with branches and vines and leaves and moss. In the night, while they were occupied near the bonfire, the jaguar, attracted by the smell of fresh meat, walked into the pit. His blood-curdling howls filled the jungle night. The gun bearers took Franc there, where the mozoes danced around, teasing the beast with long sticks, and were ready for her to take the final shot. But she could not to do it.

> *I could not bear to shoot it thus, in cold blood, with no opportunity to fight back. I have never cultivated that type of sportsmanship and so the head hunter used his ancient firearm, soon quieting the calls that had echoed these many hours.*

So ended her first trip to Quirigua. As we have seen, when she visited there again, it was with archaeologist George Gordon.

Chapter 10
THE MINISTERING ANGEL

At the time of Will's death in 1910, someone who wrote an "appreciation" of Franc called her a "Ministering Angel." This image emerged early in their time in Guatemala. Indeed, a portion of every day in Franc's life in the jungle seemed to be spent in caring for the sick or injured - both animal and human. As noted earlier, I have not been able to find any information about how she acquired these skills. She did not seem to have formal training - certainly it was not part of the curriculum at Monticello Seminary. Very likely, at that time in history when much health care occurred in the home and doctors made house calls, she was able to observe their methods and probably assist them. She had a keen interest in the subject and certainly much curiosity. During the four years after she graduated from Monticello and lived in Denver before marrying Will, she had opportunities to observe doctors as they visited family members. That was the time when her ailing brother, Tom, came to Denver from Illinois, hoping the mountain climate would help cure his TB. He stayed with the Pennebakers and Franc would certainly have visited frequently. In one of Will's letters to Franc when he was courting her, he commented on her anxiety over her brother and tried to cheer and comfort her.

If there is such a being as a "born nurse," Franc seems to have been one. Someone has described the quality as a "personal well of caring" that drives some people to want to tend the sick and to be able to do it competently and reassuringly. Franc took seriously each case that came her way and approached it with a professionalism that would have done credit to a modern day trained health care worker. But she had no formal training and no official credentials and, though she spent many hours with some of the patients, she was not paid for this work while in Guatemala - other than with gifts bestowed by grateful patients or their families.

We have noted earlier that she had been in Chicago at the time of the Columbian Exhibition in 1893 and may have attended the meeting that has been referred to the "coming out" of the nursing profession. On the other hand, her being there at the time was probably one of those interesting coincidences that occur from time to time.

As early as 1899, Franc had written in a letter to the Susans that:

> *I try to look after the sick in the camps and the natives as well who apply to me and I hear I have gained the reputation of being the best doctor on the line - but that is a bit of sarcasm, I assure you.*

As they settled into their jungle home in 1900, there was no shortage of "cases" to test Franc's skills. There were all the usual injuries to be expected in a logging camp. Some happened because of accidents with the equipment they used. Many seemed to be caused by the ever-present machetes - that essential tool of jungle life. When the men in the camps got into fights, they often escalated into "machete play" and blood flowed. In her diary, she noted the injuries.

> *Dressed Hernandez' hand which was cut open by a machete.*
> *Treated the Section boss's foot - washed it in sheep dip.*
> *Went to dress Neal's foot. It was something awful.*
> *Dressed hand of a boy - palm had been cut open.*
> *Man had bad blow from a falling limb.*
> *Brakeman on the train got his arm crushed to splinters - I stopped the bleeding and kept him quiet til the doctor came. He died the next day.*
> *Saw woman with bad ear, man with bad toes, boy with very bad hand.*

The word seemed to spread about the area that the "patrona" at the Big House could cure illnesses with her foul-tasting medicines. (Franc's comment in one of her diaries was that the natives were more apt to believe the medicine would work if it tasted terrible.) At the logging camps, there were outbreaks of malarial fever and she often sent medicine for that as well as for aching gums and teeth, cuts between toes, eye problems, wound infections and hookworm. Franc had a preferred way of treating malaria - instead of using quinine, she used calomel and in one of her diaries, she gave an explanation which she attributed to a Dr. S. Sullivan Stewart.

Calomel does not act as such but must first be changed in the alimentary tract into grey oxide and other soluble forms of mercury. In the space of two or three hours the rest of a large dose is evacuated unchanged and without having produced any result whatever. For this reason, it is probable that poisoning cannot be produced by a single dose of calomel no matter how large it might be. Repeated small doses produce the maximum effect of this drug.

Franc acquired a reputation beyond her plantation for her treatment of hookworm, so much so that it was eventually noticed by President Cabrera himself. He wrote a letter of commendation which was sent to an official named Chandler and passed on to her in 1910. She wrote that she used a combination of thymol, salts and valeriano which was, apparently, quite effective.

In addition to the native workers, a number of expatriates - those working in the coffee, mahogany and banana businesses and their wives and children - came to Franc. There were not many doctors available and word spread that Mrs. Brown could help. While they were living in the jungle, section bosses and company managers came to her when their bouts of fever raged. Mr. Guthrie of the Chambers, Guthrie Co. spent some days in their home suffering with 105 fever. Other names were mentioned as being under her care when their fevers raged - Klanke, Melville, Don Arturo, Jekyll, deMoye.

In her 1900 diary, Franc wrote a list of the various medicinal combinations that she used when a sick or injured person came for help. She seems to have kept them on hand at whichever home she occupied. Included are:

Tinctures - valarian, belladona, digitalis, aconite, arnica, iodine, nux vomica; acids - carbolic, tartaric; scillac syrup; strychnin hydroxide; ipecac; eucalyptus oil; essence of peppermint; paregoric; peroxide; chloroform; epsom salts; fruit salts; laudanum; glycerine; ammonia; vaseline - and many others.

Fruit salts - which I confess to never having heard of before reading her diaries - is extravagantly touted in a large advertisement in the Letts diaries. Eno's Fruit Salt will "prevent any over-acid state of the blood." It also will prevent and remove diarrhea in the early stages, as well as being a treatment for scarlet fever, small pox, measles and gangrene! It was noted that..

> *...without such a simple precaution, the jeopardy of life is immensely increased.*

A professional nurse stated that she has been in the business for ten years and due to Eno's Fruit Salt has not been ill for a single day!

If Franc were a physician, it could be said that her "practice" grew through the years as her reputation spread. After 1905, Will and Franc began to move away from the mahogany business and spent more time at their Tameja *finca* on the Rio Dulce nearer to Livingston. There she tended more people, both natives and ex-pats, and talked about visiting her patients every day - making her "rounds."

> *Began treating Mexican with an immense sore on his skin for 8 months.*
> *Went to Coolie Hill with medicine for child and mother and food for starving baby.*
> *Little native child came with little brother to be taken care of.*
> *One woman came with 7 month old baby like a little old woman's mummy.*
> *One of Mr. K's Jamaicans cut his throat and was brought to town. He is crazy and has to be tied down. We are looking after him.*
> *Took a walk to Indian houses near Jocolo and found 2 or 3 or 4 sick in everyhouse.*

After 1907, when Will was appointed British vice-consul for the area, they spent time both at Tameja and in the consul house in Livingston. Their life involved far more socializing. People visited frequently and they entertained often with drinks and meals. It was all much more "civilized" then the Big House in the jungle. As the years passed, Franc and Will felt stresses in their relationship; they quarreled frequently and

Franc was sometimes anxious and unhappy. Yet she continued caring for her patients without stop. Whatever was going on at home, however distressed and worried she might be personally, she made her daily patient visits and her description of one of them shows her kindness and patience.

Franc began to see an old woman - Nan - who had a wound that had not been treated and had become infested with maggots. There was no one to care for her and when Franc began to visit, she was in a very serious condition. Franc began to go every day to her little hut to try to treat the wound and remove the maggots. She noted that the smell was appalling and she had to stop frequently and go outside to be sick. But she kept at it, patiently picking the worms out, cleaning the wound, and attending to her needs. In spite of Franc's efforts, the woman died. Yet she spent her last days in greater cleanliness and comfort than she would have experienced without Franc's care.

Later, we will see that these nursing experiences had prepared her for jobs that could support her as a widow with little income. In Miami and Memphis, she was able to find work caring for sick people in their homes and for morphine addicts attempting to kick their habit. It was difficult, unpleasant, even dangerous work but it supported her for a time in her desire to live an independent life.

Chapter 11
TWO PLANTATIONS

For six years, Will and Franc continued to work in the mahogany forests. However, in March of 1903, Franc wrote that Will and Jekyll went to Livingston and bought the "Adams property," and registered the titles in Zacapa. This was the land that became their Tameja banana plantation, although they did not give up the mahogany work entirely until 1907. In buying this property, they were very likely responding to what was becoming the demise of the mahogany trade in Central America. Its peak had been the last quarter of the 19th century and by this time, African mahogany was beginning to dominate the market. It was a smart move to buy their own land and look toward the lucrative banana trade.

There was talk in early 1903 of war with Salvador and Honduras. The rumor was that the government was taking animals and men for the troops in case of need. Franc noted that in February there were 35,000 troops at the frontier and that when the train went down, it carried General Drummond to command them. In March, she and Will went to Guatemala City and met with Arathoon and Pierce of Chambers, Guthrie and, along with learning that they must leave their current home, enjoyed some splendid meals and went to a concert. Their return home was an eventful trip that involved riding on mules as well as on the train and staying overnight at Gualan and Port. At home, they found great disorder because of a storm that had blown down cattle sheds and trees.

But there was little time to waste on repairs to the damage. There followed several days of constant packing and re-arranging of their affairs in preparation for moving. Franc wrote nothing else in her diary until October when her only comment about her new home was:

> *This is the first time I ever tried keeping house on the retail plan and I don't know how to go about it.*

It is not clear where they moved though Franc's comments about the "retail plan" may suggest some uncertainty about supplies and provisions. But her references to the camps nearby and the work that is being done and the people they see and their travels here and there indicate that they were still in the vicinity of the Motagua River and the narrow gauge railroad that ran near the border of Honduras. They still seem to be overseeing the same camps - Andes, Morales, Vigia. Buena Vista. Most of the people involved in the work are the ones we have met before, though new ones appeared frequently, with no information as to who they were or what work they were doing. When she wrote to the Susans that June, she said,

I have moved - but nowhere in particular.

Franc began to mention the Potts and the Swifts often in her diary - names that would appear much more frequently later. They were Americans who had lived in Guatemala for a number of years though it is not clear why they had settled there. The Swifts eventually returned to the States and Franc visited them after Will's death at their home in Georgia. Lucy Potts eventually became Franc's closest friend. She and her husband owned property in Izabal as well as a large and beautiful home, Jocolo, on the shore of the lake. They had been in Guatemala for 36 years and for a long time, were the only white people there. Franc was to spend many days at Jocolo after Will's death and would later make long visits to Lucy at her home in Miami.

In late 1903, Franc began to mention her photography which became an absorbing hobby. Though deteriorated over time, the photos which she took and learned to develop herself give us a picture of her plantation homes and the huts and shackalows at the mahogany camps and banana groves. We see her riding the push cars on the railroad, swimming in the rivers, playing with the animals in her zoo and enjoying the interiors of her various homes. There are pictures with the guests who often visited and she was usually the only female anywhere to be seen. She included several in her letter to the Susans and remarked that a professional had told her they were quite good.

1904 - Visitors from Home

In the spring of 1904, Franc's sister, Sallie Pennebaker, and three of her children came from Kentucky to visit and were there for two months. For my own father, Howard, it was an unforgettable experience that he mentioned often later in life. But Franc wrote of it only in passing in her diary. Between descriptions of loading cattle, the arrival of boats and trains, keeping track of supplies, the new United Fruit Company steamer, storms that blew through often, she noted that Sis (her usual name for Sally) and the children went to the Circus or went swimming. Along with Howard, there were two of Sally's other children - Ruth and Charlie. The older son, Eugene, was in school and could not join them. Franc mentioned that they celebrated Howard's birthday on April 13 - he was 12.

Howard, Charlie and Ruth Pennebaker, Sis's children

While they were visiting, Franc seemed to do more entertaining - she mentioned having "my set" for dinner. There were walks, swimming trips and circus visits. In a letter to the Susans, she said she was teaching them all to lead a healthy life.

They go barefooted and wear wipils or as few clothes as possible.
..It seems very strange to have children in the house. We have no

> *chance to get lonesome now. We really are a family of two - but now we are up to 11 or 12 (including servants.) And visitors come and go. ..They all made a trip to the end of the line....The children talked about all the alligators they had seen.*

But the busy affairs of managing the home and business occupied most of Franc's journal pages. At the end of April, the Pennebaker family returned to the States and Franc went back to running the plantation. They were clearly still involved with mahogany, mentioning the cattle and mules and muddy tracks and the beaters working on the logs. But she also began to write about bananas and visits to Tameja. In May she wrote that Klanke had shipped 4500 bunches from Tameja Fruit Co. - the largest shipment by one person or company. Klanke was not one of the original owners but appears to have been hired to help manage the banana business while Will and Jekyll (the actual owners) continued working with mahogany. This involvement of Klanke was the beginning of a business tangle that would not end until long after two of the three were dead!

Franc saw the Potts often. Mr. Potts was quite sick. Franc and Agatha (her longtime servant and lifelong correspondent) were taking turns staying with him at night and were trying to get him well enough to go to the States for treatment. Eventually he did get on board the *Anselm* and on his way.

There was frequent movement between Tameja and the mahogany camps In June there were several big floods in the river and Franc was much frightened on one of their trips upriver. They stayed at the camp in June, celebrating the 4th of July by putting up the flag and decorating the posts of the veranda with cocoa palms. People stopped in frequently. As the summer wore on, there was constant rain and the river was high as the logs were sent down. Some of Franc's beloved animals were sick - a couple of them died with a mysterious illness in which they "could not control their jaws" and had very high fevers. She also noted that her little deer had died.

One of President Cabrera's innovations was the annual celebration of the feast of Minerva. It happened in October and was an excuse for merriment - another fiesta to celebrate. In November, Jekyll bought a new boat, a gasoline-powered launch that he named *Mariposa*. Other boats that plied the river were mentioned daily - the *Carib*, the *Quetzal*, the *Belize*, the *Barrios*.

North Front St., Belize.

A street in Belize

December brought the annual trip to Belize for the holidays and the hiring for the coming year. It had become, over their five years there, something of a vacation, a respite from life in the jungles. Belize, though small in comparison to other Crown Colonies, had all the trappings of king and empire, including orderly, civilized government and a gentrified social life. It was a contrast to the frequent upheavals in Guatemala with its threatened revolutions and subsequent crackdowns. In Belize, there was the Polo Club, some pleasant hotels and entertainments such as theater and concerts. Among Franc's memorabilia are programs from dances and "At Homes" and several dinner invitations to Government House, spanning the years 1903 to 1908. Several friendly notes to her were from the governor's wife, Mrs. Wilson. After Will's appointment as Consul - if not before - they would have had an entree into the best clubs and homes. So this annual winter visit was a "re-fuelling" for them while they exercised their main activity there - the hiring of the mahogany crews.

Finishing with mahogany

By 1905, the Browns seem fully involved in both the mahogany work and the banana plantation with houses at both locations. When they returned in January from the winter visit to Belize, they took a boat up to the camps and found the river in top gallant flood. Friends - the Parhams and the Swifts - visited them there and before long, strangers who needed rooms and had been sent by Mrs. Norich came up also. They were insect collectors from Indiana who remained for a week. One was a druggist; one was a clerk in a bank. Not long after they left, Hallam, a collector of birds and mammals, from Chicago arrived. He was on the hunt for manatees and was soon joined by others who had the same interest.

In contrast to their earlier isolation, the Browns were constantly visited during this period. Those who frequently joined them for dinner included Evans of the United Fruit Company, Ross, Klanke, Melville, Reed, Don Manual and even some women - Mrs. Knight and Alice and Mrs. Norich. The Noriches were long time residents of Livingston and apparently were known by everybody in the area. They had a store and a cafe and bar and when Mr. Norich died in March, there was a mass and service at the church, which everyone, including the Browns, attended.

There was a dance at the Custom house in March and President Cabrera

..took his seat for a second term of 6 years without any trouble.

Indeed - who would dare to cause any?

Franc seemed busy that year with her house and commented that she "overhauled under the house" and also redid the sitting rooms and put an outside cover on a chair. She cleaned two spare rooms, put up clean curtains, laid a new mat and put fresh ruffles on the bed. But it isn't clear which house she is writing about and where - is it the one near the mahogany camps at San Francisco or is it Tameja? Though she talked about Tameja, they did not seem to be living there on a permanent basis.

But she seemed to be constantly re-arranging whichever house they were living in, partly due to frequent guests who used their bedroom while she and Will moved to another.

Photographs of the inside of Franc's houses indicate that they were not really living in primitive conditions and had managed to acquire a number of civilized amenities. There is a piano which, she noted in a diary entry, Will played from time to time. There is a photograph of Will's study with a large roll-top desk very much like one advertised in the Letts Diaries. No doubt Franc perused those ads on a regular basis and kept up with new products on offer. She eventually ordered a typewriter which she taught herself to use. And there were always ads for medicines - Freeman's Chlorodyne, Whelpton's Purifying Pills ("invaluable for ladies") - not to mention Eno's Fruit Salts, mentioned earlier. Thus, they kept up with the larger world and tried to be part of it.

Klanke, who was still managing Tameja, was quite ill with fever in April and stayed with the Browns while Franc nursed him. His recovery was slow - she remarked that he was out all the time but did not eat and had a terrible cough. She noted that there was plenty of sickness around and mentioned giving medicine to Don Arturo and to an old woman and to Klanke's boy and doctoring the cooks' eye. Neal, one the black workers, had been attacked by a shark which badly injured his foot and she cared for him.

> *It was something awful.*

In May, she wrote that she herself felt ill, and had not rested well all week. Franc's usual energetic spirit seemed to be flagging. She said that she

> *...could not sleep, felt bad and worried, and cannot stop.*

A few days later, she noted that the depressed feeling had lifted. But a little later, she developed a sore on her ankle that was very painful and caused her to limp around for almost a month. She finally saw a Dr. Peters who dressed and treated it and by June, it was much better. Through it all, Franc continued to care for guests, including

Mr. Guthrie from the mahogany company who was suffering from persistently high fevers.

And there were the usual daily hazards of life at the camps. Franc took a walk in a graveyard and was badly bitten by red bugs and ticks. She wrote,

> *Having a terrible time!*

Someone stole the axle caps off the "American truck" and when they were replaced by spares, those were stolen also so the truck could not be used. Will smashed his fingers badly while loading cattle.

But in the midst of all this sickness and gloom, there were some bright moments. Franc was busily acquiring orchids to send to Mrs. Guthrie in London. Three boxes arrived in May; she had been trying for two years to get them. Soon she had 165 ready to go and shipped them off, via Belize. In April, Franc wrote that they were invited to go to lunch aboard an Atlas Line ship in the harbor - the *Gracia*. She wrote that they had an--

> *..A1 lunch and all the best to drink.... There was a band and*
> *we danced and everyone got a load on and we had a high old time.*

She sent the captain some flowers the next day and he wrote her a note of thanks and sent his card.

In May, Franc talked about several cases of yellow fever - or what appeared to be yellow fever - in Belize and worried that it would spread to their area. Apparently there was much concern about Puerto Barrios and boats had been ordered not to take passengers to several ports in the area. At this point in time, people still believed that yellow fever was contagious and were much concerned. Franc wrote to the Susans that there had been a quarantine and complained that she had never been "corralled" for so long. When they went to Belize, they had to go by way of New Orleans!

Speaking of illnesses, she remarked to Maud in the Susans letter ....

> *I am like you, too practical to believe in anything as intangible as CS. I believe a whole lot in the "power of mind over body" - when the problem is mental or nervous - but no more.*

Assuming that she is referring to Christian Science, we shall see how her beliefs about that changed over the next few years.

She continued to enjoy swimming and jumped off the wharf at Tameja regardless of the alligators swimming around. They caught sharks weighing as much as 110 pounds. They also caught an alligator, saving his skin for bags, his fat to be used as needed, the meat for the dogs.

Franc used her code more often than usual in this diary and as we have noticed, it was primarily to describe a problem relating to Will. His drinking worried her but they also seemed to quarrel frequently and she felt a coldness from him at times that had not been there before. This was something new in her writings and, it seems, in their relationship. It was a foretaste of what was to come over the next few years.

By this time, Franc and Will had been married for 10 years. March 4 was their anniversary but she remarked that they did not celebrate on that day but would do so the next. She began to write more often in her code and in May she said:

> *Mr. B said things to hurt me. I had a terrible time.*

Chapter 12
VISITING IRELAND

After eleven years in the tropics, Franc and Will were more than due for a change. There had been, of course, the periodic hiring trips to Belize which offered more sophisticated companionship and entertainment than existed in Livingston or Port. And there were the train trips to Guatemala City where they found some pleasant restaurants and theatrical or musical entertainment and more varied shops. But, in all that time, they appear to have left the country only once - to go to the States in 1902 to visit Franc's family. And there is no indication that Franc had ever met Will's family or been to their home. So, in the spring of 1906, they sailed for England and from there, to Ireland. Unfortunately, whatever diary Franc may have kept or whatever letters she may have written to friends and family during that visit have not been found. What we do have is photographs she took and a number of post cards she collected to suggest to us what she saw and did while there.

It was the Edwardian Age in England, a time when Britannia still ruled the waves and the sun never sat on the Empire. The aristocracy still had great wealth and political influence and carried on the social habits and rituals they had long enjoyed - weekends at country estates with riding, hunting and lawn tennis - and elegant dinners in their city homes with dances and evenings at the opera. They were living in what has been called "the long, Edwardian summer." Will's family in Ireland were landowners and though not quite of Downton Abbey caliber, were considered the landed gentry. They were, in a modest way, a part of the upper class. If her experience in 1906 was anything like what she described in her diary of eight years later, she got a taste of this good life.

Will's home was in Cashel in county Tipperary. Tipperary is the largest inland county in Ireland and has traditionally been known as a cattle-breeding area. It is also great country for breeding horses and dogs. Though not on the sea, it boasts some lovely waterways, notably the river Suir and the lake Lough Derg. The Galtee mountains rise to the south and they, along with the rich hills and valleys - the Golden Vale of Tipperary - make for a splendid natural setting. Historically, it is most famous for the Rock of Cashel, sometimes called the Acropolis of Ireland. It rises from the surrounding plains to a height of 200 feet and is crowned by a magnificent group of ruins, site of the reign of the Kings of Munster for seven centuries. Here is where St. Patrick is said to have plucked a shamrock to hold up as an explanation of the Trinity. Chief among the ruins are the 90 foot round tower, the ruined cathedral, Cormac's Chapel and the Cross of Cashel.

Will's family consisted of his brother John, and three sisters - Effie, Lil and Maud. On the tombstone which Franc erected in Guatemala, it is noted that Will was born at Fort Edward, Cashel, on June 16, 1867. John had remained on the estate and seemed to be managing it and Lil and Effie were living there also. A third sister, Maud, had married and had moved off the estate.

What we know about this visit can be inferred from looking at the pictures Franc took while on this trip. Postcards from John to Will in March of 1906 picture the new railway station at Cashel ("What do you think of it?") and the Bishop's Palace in Cashel ("Your visit will never come quickly enough!") Franc took photographs of John and Will in top hats; of Will with tennis racket accompanied by a young girl, possibly one of the sisters and another with a slim young woman, perhaps Franc herself. Other photographs are of Will on horseback with several other riders on what must have been a hunt - in one of them, a pack of dogs are sniffing among the rocks. Other pictures portray the family among the ruins, seated on the grass at the base of the Tower or admiring the cross of Cashel. A frequent scene was the Palace of Cashel, a splendid Queen Anne house built by an archbishop in 1730 and surrounded by a lovely garden. (This has become a grand hotel.)

If Franc's visit to the family after Will's death is any indication, this 1906 visit was full of social engagements. There were garden parties, tennis tournaments, golf games, dinners, and teas. No doubt every possible effort would have been made to welcome the long absent brother and his bride. Certainly, Franc would have been impressed. In spite of her fondness for swimming with alligators and welcoming deer at her dining table in the jungle, there was that other side of her which enjoyed parties, loved beautiful clothes and dressing up, and was quite happy (for awhile) socializing with the mighty.

She enthused over the trip in her letter to the Susans, saying,

> *I love their brogue with its expressions and accents, it is just delicious.!*

But there were a few problems, too. One of Will's sisters, Maud, had a baby and another of the sisters went to stay with her. Then the remaining sister got very sick - all on the same day, while Will ("my good man") was out fox hunting. So Franc was left with nursing and housekeeping. We shall see that when she refers to him as "my good man," she means he is anything but!

Franc's portrait, made in London, 1906

After the visit in Ireland - or perhaps before (it isn't clear) - they spent several weeks in England seeing the sights. Because of the postcards that she saved, we can assume that they spent some time in London - seeing

Hyde Park, St.Paul's, Trafalgar Square, Parliament, Whitehall, the Tate, Leicester Square, St. James Park, the Admiralty Arch. They probably also visited Winchester Cathedral and Sheffield and Kent. There are several postcards of the West Sussex area - Arundel Castle and Brighton and a few that depict the beach and town at Littlehampton. When she traveled to England after Will's death, Franc was entertained and hosted by Mrs. Spencer - she of the rather awful yacht trip that introduced the Browns to Guatemala. It is possible that Franc and Will were also entertained by her this time. It had been eight years, after all, since the voyage on the *Republic*, and for Mrs. Spencer, Guatemala may have been far in the distant past.

Franc and Will enjoyed the amenities of continental life for six months or so. Franc noted at the beginning of her 1907 diary that they arrived in Port after -

> *...more than six months traveling in the British Isles and Jamaica en route over and the U.S. returning.*

We know nothing about their Jamaica stopover but they were met in New York by two of the Susans and visited them briefly. As they returned to the tropics, embarking on what would turn out to be their last two years together, they were about to experience major changes - in their status, in their business, in their homes, and in their relationship with each other.

Chapter 13
BANANALAND

Franc noted that on January 8 of 1907, they moved bag and baggage to Tameja to "take root." Instead of felling mahogany trees, they would be cutting bananas. Instead of traveling in a variety of locomotives, they would move everywhere by water. Tameja was nine miles up the Rio Dulce from the harbor at Livingston and the arrivals and departures of river boats were daily occurrences, just as the arrivals and departures of trains had been in the mahogany jungles. All kinds of boats plied the waters of the river - lighters, tenders, dories, pitpains, steamers, launches - and Franc knew them all by name, referring to the Carib, the Quetzal, the Tameja, the Barrios, the Belize, the Esperanza, the Vera Paz, the Coreo.

As we have seen, the transition from mahogany to bananas had begun to occur before they left for England. Having bought the property in 1903, Will and Jekyll had decided to cultivate it as a banana plantation. It was the period when United Fruit was making huge inroads in Central America and bananas were a guaranteed source of income.

It is at this time that Klanke's name appears much more frequently in Franc's writing. It is not clear whether he, too, had been involved in the mahogany business but Will and Jekyll had chosen him a couple of years before to oversee the banana plantation at Tameja. The details of their original agreement are murky but it seems that while Will was traveling in Ireland in 1906, Jekyll allowed Klanke to assume a larger role in the business and he began to see himself as a part owner. When Will returned and assumed his role as co-owner, this became a serious problem. Klanke believed that in exchange for his managerial duties, he was entitled to a 1/3 ownership. There had been verbal promises and actual promissory notes signed and things were in a "tangle," as Franc noted. The situation continued to fester long after Will's death, adding to the difficulties Franc would have in inheriting the *finca* and the business.

Tameja *finca*

At Tameja, life for Franc assumed a quieter, more domestic aspect than had been the case in the mahogany forests. With the help of her Jamaican and Carib house boys and gardeners, she got to work cleaning and whitewashing and settling into her home. Ever active, she sewed and gardened and watched over a menagerie of fowls - turkeys, cocks, ducks, geese, hens. She entertained a constant stream of guests, remarking that..

> *We keep open house and I take them all in - the invited and the uninvited. I don't mind as long as my health, strength, disposition and where-with-all holds out.*

Franc reported regularly on the banana cutting but did not seem to have the responsibility she had had in the jungles to see that provisions and equipment were available for the workers. Natives who lived in the area were employed in the cutting and remained in their homes. The cutting took place at several locations throughout the *finca*, one often mentioned being Coolie Hill.

Though Franc seemed to have less day to day involvement with the bananas than she had had with the mahogany cutting, she clearly understood how the business worked and after Will's death tried to carry it on herself for a brief period. As with the mahogany, she wrote an article about it, calling it "Romance and Courage in Bananaland." It appears not to have been published but is an enlightening description of the whole process - which involved being a small but necessary cog in the huge banana machine of the United Fruit Company. Whatever the Browns harvested at their *finca*, they sold to the Company when the steamer of the Great White Fleet arrived once a week at the port of Livingston. Franc described that scene from the barracks on the bluff overlooking the river and bay.

> *Steam tugs in the lead, followed by gasoline launches, each nearly hid from view by the great lighters, piled high with their green cargo, each giving a tow to many and varied smaller craft - wooden lighters, barges, pit-pans, dories - big and small - loaded with their quota of fruit, from several hundred bunches to only half a dozen. This string of boats overtook and passed the sailing vessels that make a start as soon as the smoke of the steamer is sighted.*

A United Fruit Company steamer of the Great White Fleet

It was first come, first served to present the bananas for inspection so it was a race for sellers to get out to the steamer early in the day. Otherwise, one waited a turn - sometimes far into the night. The bananas were inspected by receivers who would quickly decide whether to accept or reject a bunch, giving all manner of absurd excuses for tossing one aside.

Those planters who had sufficient fruit to have a contract with the UFC were paid 30 cents a bunch. Those not under contract got 25 cents. The Browns, since they had their own launch, the *Lydia,* and a schooner, the *Eliza,* bought and transported fruit from smaller farms that varied from one acre to several hundred. These planters dotted the shores of the river all the way up to Lake Izabal, sixty miles away. On the days just before the UFC steamer was to arrive in Livingston, the Browns would start upriver with launch and schooner, stopping at all the farms on one side of the river and spending the night in a tiny shack at the edge of Lake Izabal. At daybreak, they began the descent, buying fruit on the other side of the river as they made their way back to the harbor.

As for the cutting itself, the work was organized by task. To get those bunches that grew 18 feet off the ground, some workers were "cutters" only. They climbed up and did the actual deed. Other workers "backed" or "headed" it out - carrying the huge bunches on their heads to the boats. The smallest of the boats used were pitpans - long flat-bottomed canoes that could navigate in the many small streams. They took the bananas to the larger vessels described by Franc in the scene at the harbor.

Franc noted in her diary in early February that..

> *...WFB goes to work every day now, receives the cash every night and keeps check on the commissary.*

The implication is that previously he had not done that and one wonders why - or what this comment actually meant. Perhaps he was just getting back into the swing of things after their year away. In this diary, Franc sometimes expressed anger or annoyance with Will, something that she rarely had done earlier, when he was always her darling Tipperary Irishman. She wrote in February:

> *Mr. B went off to work and did not say so much as Adios. I was in a tantrum because he gave a paddle to Cornelia to go off to town.*

He seemed to be drinking more heavily. She often commented on how much he had, writing in her code. If he stopped for awhile, she commented on that, also in code. She began to use the code much more frequently and it was almost always when she wrote about his drinking or described a quarrel they had. By this time they had been married for 12 years. They had had no children but Franc, in her writings, never expressed any feeling about this. We have no idea whether it was their choice to be childless or whether there was a physical problem that prevented them from becoming parents. We remember that she told her friends years before in Mexico that she would not have a child as long as they lived in the jungle, far from access to doctors. Perhaps they felt that they were still in in that situation. As for their relationship, they had seemed, overall, loving and compatible with each other for the first ten years of their marriage. Franc never wrote anything to indicate otherwise. They worked together as a congenial team, Franc being ready to enter into any new adventure and try any new scheme.

She enjoyed being Will's right-hand man, his best friend, his invaluable aide, and expressed this repeatedly in the articles she wrote later about their life together.

But we have nothing in writing by Will to show what he was feeling by this time. Perhaps Franc's strength and determination and relentless energy were a bit overwhelming. In 1907, men were still accustomed to submission in their wives. Perhaps he began to wish for a quieter, more docile companion. Perhaps he saw her as a nag.

Or perhaps their problems, such as they were, were simply the result of their very stressful life with its financial uncertainties, isolation from society and constant exposure to illnesses, injuries and life-threatening dangers. There can be little doubt that the thorny business relationship with Jekyll and Klanke was a great worry to Will. At any rate, it is clear that his drinking was becoming a problem in 1907 - and, as it escalated through the next two years, Franc could not resist verbalising her concern about it. Writing in the diaries was probably something of an outlet for her frustration.

Throughout 1907, Will was sick rather often - on two occasions he suffered from boils - "Job's comforters," as Franc called them. She nursed him through more than one bout with those, each lasting several days. There were also the episodes of malarial fever which he suffered periodically, as did Franc and other expats. On one occasion, Will smashed his thumb and it was badly swollen. Overall, it seemed that there were a number of days when he was not able to go to the plantation.

Yet, apparently, the work did not suffer. Some days, Franc noted in her diary the number of bunches cut - 500 in February was noted as "fairly good cutting." In March, 700 was mentioned as "very good." In May, she noted 800 and in June, "the largest shipment we have ever had so far." From time to time, Franc joined Will on the weekly trips upriver to buy from other planters but she does not appear to have done this on a regular basis.

They had guests at the *finca* frequently and saw the Potts family often. Mr. Potts had died before the Browns left for England but his wife remained in Guatemala and over the next few years, was Franc's closest friend. Franc noted in May that Mrs. Potts had moved bag and baggage to Jocolo, after having lived at Izabal for over 30 years. As their friendship grew, Franc began to call her Lucy and after Will's death, she spent a great deal of time at Jocolo, Lucy's large and lovely plantation home on the banks of the lake. It seems odd, in our casual age, that one continued to call a friend of several years, "Mrs." but that was usual then. Calling her "Lucy" suggests that there was a special closeness and affection between them by this time.

Lucy's daughter - also Lucy - was a frequent visitor at Franc's home. She had recently become engaged and was very much in love. Another girl, Clara, appeared for a visit with Franc in early 1907. She, too, was in love and the two entertained Franc with their youthful antics - sometimes being in tears over their romances, at other times in ecstacies. Franc taught Clara to sew and she managed to finish a dress and start on another one. To Lucy, Franc became something of a confidante. There were frequent letters from her - to which Franc sometimes responded with a "long lecture."

Franc enjoyed the company of the young people - after all, she herself was not yet forty. When they were at Tameja, they all, with the dogs, took long walks through the *finca*. Whitman, Lucy's lover, gathered some longhaired ferns for Franc. Lucy and Whitman went fishing and came back with a bucketful - they said they even caught some with their hands! They all enjoyed weighing each other from time to time - though Franc was chagrined that she weighed the most - at 177 1/2. She often recorded her weight through the years and she does seem to be at a high point in these last 3 years in Guatemala Her usual adult weight was around 150 so she was never a small woman - though, in her articles, she enjoyed writing as if she were. She sometimes referred to herself as a "slip of a girl" and talked about "stamping her little foot."

Franc reading while floating in the Tameja creek

Among Franc's favorite activities was swimming and there was certainly plenty of water around in which to indulge her fondness for it. Unfortunately, the rivers and streams were rife with other swimmers - alligators, snakes, piranhas. But not to be deterred, she got her houseboys to chase them away while she floated on her back reading a book! Franc continued to experiment regularly during this period with her photography and couldn't resist a picture of that activity. She was using one of the early Kodak cameras and did her own developing. She wrote in March..

I tried to develop a roll of films in the back room last night in abbreviated attire but the whole film was a failure, light got to it.

Many of the pictures she took at this time were developed on what looks like post cards. She printed 68 in late May and noted that she was sending prints and films to the "Kodak people."

Rumblings began to be heard from Jekyll. Whatever had happened between him and Will on Will's return from abroad, Jekyll had not been on the scene at Tameja since their arrival there in January. In March, Will got a letter from him demanding to see all papers and contracts regarding the Tameja Fruit Co. In Livingston, there was a dust-up at the local store when Jekyll confronted Klanke there about Tameja affairs. There was, Franc noted, a "hellava row." Klanke then gave Jekyll "particular hell" in front of a bar room full of people. The next day, a letter arrived for Will from Klanke asking Will to come to town at once as he refused to deal with Jekyll. Will said he would not go until the books had been brought up to date which would not be until April.

So things simmered on for several days. Then came a letter from Jekyll that he was going to Morales to bring back all book accounts and prove he does not have to pay his promissory note. He remained testy, seizing on every opportunity to quarrel with Will and claiming damages for delay and "waste of time" in not being able to settle.

In late March, news came to Franc and Will by way of the boats that put in daily that natives were being rounded up to fight in case of revolution or attack. One of their plantation people, Fernando, was made a sergeant and other native men were taken. When the Browns made a visit to Port on the *Quetzal,* they found that there were three steamers waiting to load bananas which..

...could do nothing on account of the revolution.

In May, they learned that there was trouble in Guatemala City, including attempts on the president's life. Franc wrote,

Awful things are going on in the city.

On the 25th, there were 150 artillary men in Livingston and they were ready to gather all men - Caribs included - in case Nicaragua attacked. In June, she noted that Puerto Barrios was full of guns and fortifications as they expected an attack at any moment. A Mexican man-o-war was expected to arrive in mid-June. The situation was *muy grave*.

Yet, as she wrote of these rumblings, Franc did not express any genuine anxiety. It was as if she did not expect the situation to affect them personally. And indeed, things simmered down before the year was over. It was all part of an incipient rebellion against the autocratic President Cabrera which had some support from neighboring countries. Cabrera, however, showing once again his talent for survival, held on for nearly 14 years longer.

There were several storms in June, with flooding and heavy winds and torrential rains. Severe earthquakes were reported in Izabal and Livingston. Franc spent a lot of time tending to her chickens and ducks who had developed all sorts of problems and were in a "bad state." Caring for the animals was an ongoing task. But there was also, for a time, a surveyor from Guatemala City who became ill and rested there in their hammock until recovered.

In spite of the sicknesses and ongoing war threats, there seemed to be some light moments. Franc remarked in late June that there is..

> *...plenty doing in the social world around here.*

They left Tameja in their "buggy" (boat) for Livingston where they went to an event at the Custom House their first night, then to an opening of a new park and bandstand. It was *fiesta* time and there was a very exclusive ball given by the *Jefe* to which very few besides the chief men of the town and their mistresses were invited. The Browns, however, were and...

> *....surprised everybody and ourselves in particular by going. I enjoyed it to a certain extent. It was a motley lot.*

During *fiesta,* all rules for good behavior were, apparently, broken. Franc commented that the administrator fell off the wharf, he was so "loco.' And, while they were there in Livingston, Klanke began a long alcoholic binge - something which seems to have recurred from time to time. Franc said that it was touched off when the *Jefe* and a crowd were in the shop - the main store and bar - and made him take a drink. Then 20 bottles of champagne were drunk.

Franc and Will had come prepared to stay in Livingston for a week or ten days as the arbitration regarding the Tameja Fruit Co. was due to happen. Various other people arrived for that, acting for the three parties - Will, Jekyll and Klanke. At first, Klanke was not visible. Then he appeared, went into a bar called Molinos and sat there until he was "paralyzed." Meantime, Jekyll, with his representative, arrived and wanted to talk but Klanke was, obviously, not ready.

On the 12th, the arbitration meeting finally occurred. Klanke did not appear and Franc wrote that there was "a high old time." The result of the arbitration was that Will was to have entire and sole charge of the Tameja Fruit Company business and was to have $150 gold as a salary. But there was further discussion in a "meeting of the clans" later in the day about how much Jekyll really owed Will who held his promissory note for $2,000. Nothing was gained and after half the night, Will finally tore up the note in disgust!

They went back to Tameja and Will immediately took his boat up river to gather fruit from the planters. The next day and several days following in July were stormy and there was much anxiety over the boats. Some had broken down and help had to be sent to bring in the men and smaller boats. Franc wrote,

> *Such awful worry and anxiety and the first trip at that.*

Klanke finally sobered up and he and Will were able to talk more sanely about their difficulties. However, Franc noted that he moved out of their house (had he been there throughout his long binge?) and she and Will were getting re-settled in their old bedroom. There was talk of other business matters, such as the warehouse they had all owned. Franc went there to look after some "kids" who were squatting there. Will urged Klanke to have the titles to it transferred to him as the new, sole owner of the business properties.

After July, Franc's notes in the diary became very erratic and we know little about the last 5 months of 1907. The diary for 1908 has not been found. At some point during that time, probably late in 1907, Will was officially appointed British Vice-Consul for the area. There is a letter dated October, 1907, from Arathoon at Chambers, Guthrie, congratulating Will on his appointment. There is also a letter to the Susans in which she mentioned his new job.

In the same letter, Franc wrote an amusing account of a hen under the house which was sitting on three kittens and wouldn't let their mother near. Franc rescued them so that they could be fed. She wrote about other animals she had in cages - a gibnut, anteater, night monkey, and possums. She remarked that she had had a lot of nursing - had to cut off a man's finger but it healed beautifully. She also remarked on her weight which had ballooned to 185.

>*I am thoroughly disgusted with myself - I hate to look at myself - I take plenty of exercise ...walk a lot, uphill and rarely have a dry thread on me - but nary a pound do I lose.*

As Vice-Consul, it was Will's job to represent Great Britain in this Caribbean area of Guatemala and in Belize and to protect and assist British citizens living in the country. When he got the position, it meant a change in their living habits and their work situation. There was a house in Livingston for the consul to live in. They still managed the plantation and still made fruit trips up the river but Will had to be available for his consular duties, often journeying to Belize and Guatemala City where he consulted with the British ambassador and other diplomats.

It is unfortunate that we do not have the 1908 diary. When we read what Franc wrote in 1909, we see that, though physically the Browns were located in the same area and though much of their work life remained the same, emotionally their situation had deteriorated. The tensions we see in this 1907 diary - the business difficulties which were not really settled with the "arbitration" decision, Will's drinking and Franc's anxiety about it - clearly increased over the coming year. And other stressful changes came as they moved into the home in Livingston and Will took on his new responsibilities.

Chapter 14
NEARING THE END

Franc's 1909 diary is painful to read. She seems deeply unhappy - sometimes almost in despair - and in a constant state of anxiety. No longer is she the adventurous partner to her handsome husband, ready to explore new lands and try new experiences, unfazed by wild animals, primitive living conditions, myriad physical dangers and weeks of isolation. Yet from a purely material point of view she was in a much more comfortable place than she had been, living most of the time in Livingston in a hilltop house, near shops and cafes and the harbor, surrounded by other people. As the vice-consul's wife, she was respected and invited to such social events as Livingston had to offer. She traveled often to Guatemala City where she got to know people in the diplomatic corps such as Godfrey Haggard, British Vice-Consul there and William Owens, American Consul. She began to develop a lasting friendship with the Irish Bellinghams who were attached to the British legation. Yet Franc was frequently miserable, obsessed with Will's drinking, his perceived unkindness to her and their bitter quarrels. She tried to find comfort in the arms of their friend, Bernard. But that offered only partial relief. She wrote in August after an evening with BZ,

I was happy, then unhappy as I am __always__ now.

Photographs show their Livingston house to be a spacious bungalow. It was surrounded by a wide porch and was on a hill with a splendid view of the harbor. Livingston is a town that climbs and every photograph - whether taken by Franc in 1909 or her nephew Charlie in 1938 or by me in 1995 - shows that steep incline from the sea, climbing past small businesses along the way - cafes, stores, bars, a hotel, a warehouse. In her writing, she often mentioned going up the hill - or down the hill - to get to the store, to dine at the hotel, to visit her patients.

The view down the hill in Livingston

In this diary, Franc mentioned people we haven't met before. Probably Franc had known them previously - the expatriate community in that part of Guatemala was not large - but living at Tameja or earlier, at the San Francisco *finca*, she saw them seldom. They became close friends only when she settled in Livingston. Primarily, they were men. We begin to hear about Doerscher, Reed, Willard, Menke, Chili - and, most frequently, Bernard Zerhullen. Franc always referred to him as BZ and he was the manager of Theimers, the main store in Livingston. These men were leading citizens of the town. The frequency of German names suggests that they were descended from the coffee planters who had come to the Petan area in the mid-19th century. They were all friends of Will and Franc and BZ was Will's diplomatic counterpart - he was the German vice-consul. As the year wore on, Franc and BZ became increasingly close friends. It was a romantic relationship and almost certainly a sexual affair, though Franc, with turn-of-the-century reticence, only hinted at that.

As we read her 1909 diary, we see that Franc's relationship with Will had worsened. They were increasingly combative and quarreled often. She began her entries with a description of a party they had attended the night before.

WFB was 'devoted' as usual and he left me alone. Then there were words as usual and we both were miserable.

Franc noted one day in June that Will was too drunk to make the trip up the river to buy fruit so she paid a man to do it for him. She wrote,

I am loco.

The man she had hired was so slow in getting the fruit back that the UFC steamer left without it. A boy who was supposed to be working for her caused her trouble by being impudent and "cussing" the other servants. She wrote in October:

Everything is out of order and at cross purposes. I am passing through a terrible time...I am frightfully nervous and miserable, am longing for some sweetness from my darling.

The next day she wrote that she and Will had a dreadful time at dinner and she cried forhours. After another party when they got home at 12 AM, Franc wrote:

It was one horrible day. The worst yet. But we calmed down and went to Tameja to remain a little. It was a second honeymoon. We both cried.

They spent a peaceful few days there at their riverside *finca* - but even as she wrote that Will was calmer and more like himself there, she also wrote,

Oh, how I miss BZ.

Clearly, she was conflicted.

Franc on the porch of their Livingston house

In Livingston, BZ was often at their home. Sometimes he and Will got drunk together. Sometimes BZ was there alone for tea and he and Franc went for long walks. On most days, Franc stopped in at his store, chatting with him and other customers. They often wrote notes to each other. Sometimes when she was angry with BZ, she asked him to give them back, but she kept several of them. In a tattered envelope are a dozen or more

> *Hope you're feeling better today.*
> *I didn't see you last night - the result was six hours of dreams of you.*
> *Thank you for asking how I find this <u>triste</u> morning. I feel quite happy and well and I hope the same for you. Your BZ*

On many days he walked her home in the evenings. There were, inevitably, a few quarrels but when they made up, she wrote,

> *Such a blissful evening. I was drunk with affection.*

As the year wore on, their affair intensified and in November, she wrote:

> *I went to sleep in a big chair and around 12:30 or 1, BZ came and stayed til 3:00. I was in a kimona and he felt of my bare flesh and we behaved very badly........BZ said "I love you - I love you - I love you." At last, after nearly two years....*

It is hard to know what she was referring to by "after nearly two years" but since she had never mentioned BZ in her diaries prior to this, it is probably the length of time since she had moved to Livingston and they had become friends. At any rate, the next day, Franc was contrite and wrote that she had a horrible nervous spell and regretted the previous night - yet wrote,

> *We had a sweet, sweet evening until 11. Such bliss!*

And where was Will? Sometimes he was off on a fruit-buying trip up the river. At other times he was in Guatemala City attending to consular business. But often he was there in Livingston at Cobar's bar, drinking with his companions, paying no attention to what Franc might have been doing - or he was simply at home suffering from the effects. On returning from a trip to the City one day, he stayed home and got paralyzed drunk - in a stupor, she wrote. And they continued to quarrel. As Christmas approached - a season for even more excessive imbibing - Will came in drunk and Franc wrote:

> *He said the worse thing ever. I was wild.*

With all this stress and anxiety, it is not surprising that Franc herself began to indulge more heavily in liquid comfort. After an evening at Cobar's, she wrote:

> *I did not know what I was doing.*

Sometimes after a blissful evening with BZ she wrote:

> *I don't remember much about it.*

After mentioning a few martinis with BZ and Willard, she wrote that she had too much last night. Yet she was all too aware that she was overindulging and from time to time noted that she was on a "temperance tack."

Otherwise, much of her 1909 diary is devoted to comments on the ships that came and went. A German steamer came in with 6,000 bags of coffee. A lighter, the *Scotia*, full of coffee and cargo from up country, was lost in the rough harbor. Squalls and high winds made sea and river traffic hazardous. Their own boat, the *Lydia,* had been damaged and was out of commission for part of November and they had to find other boats for the fruit trips.

Will, when not sailing upriver with the bananas, had his consular duties to perform. One of them was to visit, as an official British representative, foreign ships that came into port. For his visit to the German steamer, Franc noted that she

> *... diked Will out complete in white to make his afternoon visit.*

He must have been handsome in the snow white uniform, tall and slim, with his dark red hair and thick mustache. But was he sober?

There is a letter to Will from Lionel Carden, the British Minister in residence in Guatemala City. He urged Will to greet and entertain a bishop from Honduras who would be in Livingston in February. And he reminded Will to be wary of a local official who seemed to be ready to disobey orders regarding the treatment of British subjects.

In mid-August Will and Franc made a trip to Guatemala City where they attended races for several days. One day they had tea at the British legation. Another night they were entertained at Delmonico's as guests of Godfrey Haggard and William Owens. Franc and some of the "young folk," then went to play roulette. But the next day she was ill with cramps and pains in her stomach. When it was time to return to Livingston, Will had to go alone as Franc was too ill to travel. She remained in the city a few more days, being visited and cared for by Mrs. Bellingham. She got better acquainted with Anne Carden, the

Minister's wife, and received a warm and friendly note from her when she returned to Livingston. These relatively new acquaintances in the diplomatic corps became loyal and supportive friends as time went on and the Browns' difficulties with the fruit company escalated.

They went back to Guatemala City again for carnival, also to a grand ball given by Mrs. Carden, at the Legation. She wrote:

> *The legation place is like a big English country house. We were there every afternoon with the officers and played outdoor games.*

Back in Livingston, in spite of her personal anguish, Franc continued to attend to several sick people. In October, a very ill Ladino woman, Anita Mason Herrara, was in Livingston. Franc visited and determined to do what she could for her, treating her with hot linseed poltices and sponge baths of rum and quinine. But Anita was too ill to be saved and died soon after being taken to Belize for help. Otherwise, there was Franc's friend, Pablo Doerscher to whom she gave quinine; Mercedes, a woman with hookworm; Anker, the former consul, who had a fever that wouldn't abate; a man named Michovsky who had taken a mysterious drug and could not be roused; Lucy Potts who came for a visit and was ill with fever while there.

Mrs. Potts stayed a few days. Then William Owens, the U.S. consul, came to town to meet his wife and daughter, Addie, who were returning from six months in the U.S. They were off the next day for Guatemala City but Franc wrote that Mrs. Owens was very sweet to her. In November, Addie came alone for a visit with Franc and stayed for several days. They seem to have been happily compatible in spite of the difference in their ages and enjoyed going for long walks along the beach and rowing on the Lake while visiting Mrs. Potts at Jocolo. Franc and Addie remained friends for many years.

An unpleasant consular duty for Will arose when he was called on to deal with a labor issue at the Virginia *finca*. There were Jamaican laborers there who had struck and there was looting and rioting. He went with soldiers on the train but came back after a few days to meet with Haggard who was coming from Guatemala City to help deal with it.

In October, there was word of a revolution in Nicaragua and Franc was very much worried - but then says no more about it. As we have seen, insipient revolutions cropped up every year or so in those Central American "republics."

And whatever had happened to Jekyll and Klanke? The ownership of Tameja was still not really settled and on November 26, Franc wrote that they got a "long, long, long horrid letter" from Klanke. She cabled for Jekyll to come out at once. It is not clear where he was at the time but he arrived in Livingston in December and began to live with them at their consul house, a not especially welcome guest. And their finances were in serious disarray. Franc wrote that on November 29, they looked at their bank debit and were in the depths of despair, seven thousand overdrawn. But how could it have been otherwise? No one seemed to be paying attention. Will was very often drunk and Franc was preoccupied with her own anguish regarding him and BZ and sometimes drowning her sorrows in the same way.

By Christmas, things were in a bad way. The servants all went home on the 23rd for their Christmas entertainment and Franc was left to serve dinner. The men (presumably BZ and Doerscher) took her out to Cobars and she went looking for Will who finally got home very drunk at 2. She wrote:

> *I was wild again,*

Thus, Christmas Eve was something of a loss but Christmas dawned a beautiful day. Will was nervous, trying not to drink. BZ, Pablo and Chili came to say Merry Christmas. Franc wrote that they got 20-25 remembrances - then added,

> *A Christmas never to be forgotten.*

On the day after Christmas, Franc wrote to the Susans - a rather sad letter.

> *I wonder if I could ever adapt to life as an ordinary human being in the States. I have many correspondents - U.S., Mexico,*

Panama, South America, Ireland, England, Germany, India, Borneo. ...I have had fever frequently but I bob up serenely as soon as the fever leaves me. Lots of guests and I have to turn our little pill box upside down and inside out to hold 5 guests. In Guatemala City for fiesta. Sat in the President's box for the races. The scene was brilliant. Many different languages floating around....Our existence here has reached rock bottom but I don't see any chance of its rising again very soon.

An arbitration with regard to Tameja was due again- but it did not happen because Klanke did not have an arbitrator. Will was ill with pains on his left side so he was not drinking at all for a few days. On New Years Eve, Franc went to a dance without him and played roulette. BZ was there but paid no attention to her - none whatever. So her final remark of the year was,

Will is so patient and good.

It appears that when one of her men was down, the other had to be up!

It is hard not wonder whether Will's behavior was brought on partly by his suspicion that Franc was having an affair with BZ. But it seems rather more likely that the affair developed in part because she was so distressed by Will's growing indifference and by his heavy drinking. Perhaps we would understand it all better if we had her 1908 diary and knew more about their move into Livingston, Will's appointment to the consular position, and how it affected their lives; perhaps if we knew more about the trip to Ireland and Will's family in 1906; perhaps if we understood more about their business affairs and conflicts over Tameja; perhaps - especially - if we had anything written in Will's words. Or - perhaps it was simply impossible to maintain even a minimally happy marriage in the circumstances in which they were living.

At any rate, it was indeed a "Christmas never to be forgotten." Before the next one rolled around, Will would be gone. And Franc would be facing dramatic, lasting changes in her way of life.

Chapter 15
THE DEATH OF WILL

There is no diary for 1910. In a letter to the Susans, dated May of that year, Franc wrote that she had been in bed with a serious attack of fever - threatened "congestion of the brain." Will was in the City and there was no servant to do anything - to even bring her a glass of water or a cup of tea.

> *I got tired of all my servants some 6 or 7 weeks ago and turned them all out - and have not tried to get others. I needed change of some sort so got rid of them. My cook, housekeeper, maid and - really - chief refuses to work for anyone else - at any kind of pay - so I think I will take her back shortly.....I have nothing but tales of woe as to our health and finances so I had better write as little as possible. I went to the city some weeks ago but my husband was all run down in health and was very ill so there was no fun in it..... My good man goes back again to the annual fiesta of horse races in August but I am like "Flora in a Flimpsy," I have nothing to wear. I have a lot of sewing and writing to pass away solitary hours. It nearly kills me to be alone. But "you can't keep a good thing down" so I "bob up serenely."*

Clearly, things had gone from bad to worse. Franc must have felt quite desperate to have gotten rid of the servants but couldn't help trying for a little humor and a stiff upper lip when writing to the Susans.

On September 19, 1910, Will died, at age 45. He was, even for that time in history, a fairly young man and, though he had been ill, his death seems to have been entirely unexpected. According to his obituary, he had been suffering from pleurisy for some time and had gone to Guatemala City for treatment. In August, he was back in Livingston much improved and making his fruit buying trips up the river. On one of them he was caught in a severe rainstorm. The exposure exacerbated his recurring lung problems. Franc's letter to the Susans was full of sorrow.

Will in Ireland, 1906

Sisters, I have the saddest, hardest news to impart that a woman who LOVES can ever have to convey to her friends.....On the 17th of September he had a severe attack of some sort, spitting clots of blood and had ice cold perspiration all night. He had a third attack on Monday and spit up blood like clockwork til he died. He had such a wild, frightened look in his eye from the first. Oh, dear ones! You know how I never left him and I cannot leave him yet so I am staying here and going on with the business myself. I am alone - in many senses. At night I have a very young native girl sleep on the floor next to my bed. That is all the companionship I have.

The obituary expressed sympathy and regret.

His loss will be deplored by a very large circle of friends and many a man who, when out of luck had never appealed to his generous heart in vain, will shed a tear of genuine grief when he learns of the decease of the open hearted, magnanimous and sympathetic Tipperary Irishman who was ever willing to help the needy out of their difficulties.... It was Mr. Brown who kept the otherwise sleepy town of Livingston alive with his infectious gaiety and ever cheerful manner. It was Mr. Brown that everyone in a bad way went to for help just as it was to Mrs. Brown they went when they were sick and neither would ever dream of refusing the aid requested. ...A friend to all, the comforter of the afflicted, frank, open-hearted and generous to a degree, Brown has received the final summons - he has left us - we shall never set eyes on his laughing face again. His wife, who idealized him, he has left behind to bemoan her fate in losing the best of husbands and to her, known along these coasts as the Ministering Angel, we extend our deepest and heartfelt sympathy...

Though Franc, at this point, may not have "idealized" him as she once had or seen him as "the best of husbands," Will's death was a tremendous blow to her. Will was buried there in Guatemala and, though there were anxious cables from her family in the states, along with suggestions that someone would come down to her, no one did. Her eldest nephew, Eugene Pennebaker, wrote that he would "give anything on earth" to be with her but was in charge of constructing an interurban rail line in Chicago. Bess's husband, Jeff Burgie, was not well and was occupied with managing his successful vinegar company. Sis's husband, Charles Pennebaker, appeared ready to go to her and wrote a long, comforting letter that showed his thorough understanding of the business difficulties she would face. He also strongly urged her to come home to her loving family. He wrote:

> *You cannot afford to throw your life away in a useless struggle down in that country. You have given to it the best years and dearest hopes of your life and leaving it, there will be ever coming back to you memories, both bitter and sweet. Time will tone down the one and may intensify the latter and still leave you with the power to live the rest of you life in peace with at least a measure of happiness.*

However, Charles did not go to Guatemala. It seems likely that Franc discouraged him; in spite of his wise advice, she was already determined to stay there and hang on to the business and manage it herself.

Franc, with her usual attention to record-keeping, typed a list of all those who sent condolence letters or cables. There is also a list of those who sent her Christmas cards in 1909 and 1910 and another one of her "Correspondents, January 1911." There are nearly a hundred names. Some are family members - Pennebaker, Burgie, Brown, Strode, Erwin. Some are old friends from the States or England - archaeologist George Gordon, Monticello classmate Hat McKeller, *Republic* shipmates the Spencers. But most names are friends and colleagues in Guatemala and Belize and are from all walks of life in that area, from consuls to native lawyers to Jewish merchants to former servants and, at the top of the list: El Presidente, Manuel Estrada Cabrera. Those were the people who made up Franc's world - more so at that point than her family and friends in the States - and she was not ready to say goodbye to them any more than she was ready to say goodbye to Will.

Of course, there were letters from Will's family. John wrote:

> *No one knows how fond I was of Will and I feel so <u>lonely.</u> Everything I did around here I used to wonder if he'd like it when he came back. Now he never will. Poor darling Will - he was such a boy.*

Effie and Maud also wrote. Effie's note included a litany of complaints about her sister, Lil, but Maud urged Franc to come for a visit and asked for some momento of Will.

> *...a book he has read...a tie - I could wear a tie ... any trifle that you won't miss.*

William Agar, a longtime Guatemala colleague, wrote:

> *I do not think he had an enemy in the world.*

(Well ... let's not forget Jekyll - or Klanke...)

There was a note to Franc from an M. Poltschbach who wrote:

> *I know you are good - the best person I know in this country. You are good to others but now you must be good to yourself.*

Of course, the Susans wrote of their concern for her and her answer to those "sweet, old-time friends" is full of her sadness. She apologized for using the machine (typewriter) to write but noted that it distracted her from her grief since she had to pay attention in order to use it. She wrote:

> *I do not know how to even begin to tear up the roots of my crushed heart, to leave this seductive land where I and mine drank so deep of the bittersweet of life for so many years. But it is inevitable and I must make a mighty effort to accustom myself to the idea.*

She went on to describe her hilltop home and her one servant who shared her meals, but notes that she had no interest in food, adding,

> *I still weigh 162 (a disgrace)so I can afford not to fret about food...*

And on a prayerful note, rather rare for her, she wrote,

> *I pray our good friend will show me my future and keep me under the shadow of his wing.*

Franc and Will had a number of friends in Belize. One who wrote to her was the wife of Rowland Ormsby, a man who will figure prominently in her life after she has left Guatemala. In London, we will meet him with his second wife and in New York, with his third.

Another who wrote was Godfrey Haggard, the British Vice-Consul in the Capital. After heartfelt expressions of sympathy, he told her that Edward Reed would take Will's place at the consulate and that Jekyll would come down and run the banana business for the time being. The latter suggestion was hardly a comfort to her as she meant to run it herself and, as we shall see, his appearance on the scene would complicate the already thorny issue of her ownership of the Tameja Fruit Company.

Along with her very real anguish over Will's death, Franc saw that she must clarify her situation with regard to the business and that she must do it quickly. We have several letters that were exchanged between her and Edward (Pat) Bellingham who had agreed, reluctantly, to act as her power of attorney in Guatemala City. He was the secretary to the British Legation there and a good friend of hers and Will's. His explanation of her difficulties was as follows.

The agreement that had been made between Jekyll and Will was to dissolve their partnership. Will was to buy Jekyll out and he was to borrow 1150 pounds from the Banco Colombiano for this purpose. This money would be available to Franc as his heir as soon as the titles to Tameja were in order. However, there were three annotations on the titles which needed to be cleared up. Two could be easily disposed of but the third, in which Klanke was still claiming part-ownership, would take some time. Pat urged Franc to come to the City with all the papers and Will's will. He particularly advised her not to try to prove the will in Livingston as it would be "interminable."

Franc seemed in no hurry to go to the City. Both Pat and Godfrey Haggard repeatedly urged her to come and told her she was welcome in their homes. They even assured her that if she was worried about having black clothes to wear, that could be taken care of "in a twinkling." Pat reminded her that she needed to settle a debt regarding the company fruit boat, the *Lydia*. If she did not make some arrangement about that, she could lose it to anyone who made a bid to cover the debt.

Haggard sent her $1,000 which he insisted was not a loan and wrote:

> *...you are only doing yourself harm and no one, not even your honourable creditors, any good by supposing you can stay in Livingston and carry on the business. To spend more money on it is only to throw it into a hole...to sell the property, settle with your creditors and still have something to start again with, will surely strike you as being the most practical plan.*

Franc refused to see this and had already begun to run the fruit trips herself. Though we don't have a diary from that time, we do have an article she wrote for possible publication which describes her activities at the time.

After I was left alone, scarcely more than a bride, I kept up the fruit shipments, without a break, believing this to be the best way to fill the vacancy that had come so suddenly and crushingly into my life, believing it to be my only salvation, not only of my peace of mind and sanity but of our interests there that we had gotten so successfully established.

In the manuscript, she went on to describe incidents that showed she could manage the workers and bring the fruit successfully to the port. She talked about doing it for "a year" but that is an exaggeration - she left Guatemala for a visit to her family within eight months of Will's death. However, for her, this activity was preferable to going to Guatemala City and dealing with lawyers and government officials. Activity - action -just doing something - was Franc's lifelong answer to sadness or anxiety.

Franc finally went to the Capital with the will, but she did not stay long. When she returned to Livingston, she continued her correspondence with Pat and her letters to him express her frustration, her anger, and her nearly despairing sadness. On her typewriter, she made copies of her frequent letters to Pat. On January 30, 1910, she wrote:

I am sorry to give you so much trouble even to read my lengthy epistles. But when I sit down to write, I am lonely as always and just talk with you on paper. I am trying so hard to be patient but it is hard for patience to "have her perfect work." I know how it is. It is impossible to get the smallest thing done here in the courts....All day today, Mr. Reed and I were trying to get a renewal of the contract Chambers Guthrie and later, my husband, had with the municipality for the ground under the warehouse and we accomplished nothing...I believe everyone is a friend of Klanke and to help me would show some crooked thing he did about getting titles and also the judge who was mixed up in it.

She went on to ask Pat to get a slab for Will's grave as quickly as possible. Then she would try to get money together for her passage and would leave the country.

> *I have prayed so earnestly that I can put all false pride aside and go to relatives and friends as best I can...I am sure I would have to be carried on the steamer unconscious.*

Later, in this long, agonized letter, she wrote:

> *I nearly faint when I realize that I am leaving him and everything forever. I really feel nearer and dearer to my good friends in this country than I do to my people, because I have been away from them so long and my interests are here and like my friends' interests and theirs are so different.*

As she concluded she wrote:

> *I am desperate. How can I do these last hard things alone? I can't bring myself to write nor talk to Jekyll but would to God someone could get him to give me $6,000 down and let him have everything and let me clear out....Please, Pat dear, pardon this long letter. I think you will not receive many more for after I am gotten rid of (to everyone's delight here anyway) the letters cannot be so frequent.*

Her grief was turning to anger and she distrusted even her close friends. On February 5, Franc wrote to Pat, noting that she planned to leave as soon as she could get ready. She was selling some things and finding it a horrible, distasteful job. She continued to express frustration at the inability to get anything accomplished with regard to her holdings. She was furious that Jekyll had appointed himself "Manager" of the fruit company.

> *I have heard people say that they do not consider him a human being so no one will recognize him in anything and they worry the life out of <u>me.</u> There is no one I can trust in the whole town.*

Going on to her anger at Klanke, she wrote of his "black schemes" and "rascality" through the years. She ended with:

I wish I could see you all, dear ones, again before I go but the going would only be harder, I suppose. I wish I could go without anyone knowing the day of my sailing for I would not like to go like I saw an old administrator of the <u>aduana</u> go from Barrios one time. He stood on the back platform of the car and waved and waved at the imaginary friends that should have been there to give him "God speed" - when there was not one person in sight to wave adieu.

We don't know who waved "adios" to Franc - but in March of 1911, she was in the States.

Home to the family

Franc going home after Will's death

Franc's letter to Pat in February seemed to be a goodbye - but not forever. At the urging of her family as well as friends in Guatemala, she made a visit to the States. Her parents had been dead for many years, as had both her brothers so her closest relatives were her sisters, Bess and Sallie (Sis). There were also cousins and nieces and nephews and aunts and uncles from both the Strode and Martin families. But, as suggested in her letter to Pat, it was a painful blow to her pride to have to go to the family for help. She, who had refused to heed their warnings about moving to the uncivilized tropics, now might have to rely on them for economic as well as emotional support. This visit to them would be a test. Could she go back to a "comfortable" life of club meetings and teas and church socials that she might find with Bess in Memphis - or to the loneliness and drudgery of farm work that she might find with Sis in Kentucky? Could she live in peace with their families, as the maiden aunt to several nieces and nephews?

On May 11, 1911, Franc began the first diary we found after Will's death. She wrote in Huntsville, Alabama where she had attended the church her father led before his early death when she was a child of two or three. She also noted that she wore a white rose for Mother's Day - remembering her mother who had died when she was 11. Her first stop on arrival in the States had probably been Bess's home in Memphis but she then began a round of visits to relatives and friends. From Huntsville, she went to Cairo, Illinois to visit Sis's family. Later in the summer, she was in Martin, Tennessee, visiting her mother's Martin relatives and from there, she headed for LaGrange, Georgia where she stayed with the Swifts, friends from her Guatemala days. Finally, in late Fall, she was back in Memphis with Bess, settling in for a long visit.

Bess's husband, Jefferson Lee Burgie - or "Brother Jeff" as Franc called him - owned a successful business that manufactured vinegar so they were financially comfortable. There were three children - J.L. Jr., Gladys and Frances - who were between the ages of 6 and 10. This visit lasted until the spring of 1912 - but there would be other lengthy stays in 1914 and 1916. Until she settled in New York in 1918, the Burgie house would be Franc's home base.

But she was hardly happy there in the winter of 1912. It was extremely cold that year in Memphis and it was hard for Franc, who had become accustomed to the steamy heat of Central America. She wrote on January 12, the coldest day on record:

My umbrella froze stiff from the car to the house.

And she was suffering from homesickness for the south. Several days had passed without mail. She wrote:

I am sick about it...the scene has completely changed from Guatemala - my cold is very fierce and I am miserable in body and mind....

I gave way to a terrible paroxysm of grief and had to go next door because the young folks were frightened....

Bess has told me all day that she is sick and tired of me. Oh, God, what shall I do?

This visit by Franc, in the first year of her grief over Will, was difficult not only for her but for those around her. It is not surprising that family members found her trying. Bess was endlessly kind and supportive but it was hard to know how to comfort Franc. And Bess had to consider her husband and three young children who hardly knew how to deal with the grieving widow. Franc's nephew, Charlie, who was in Memphis and visited often seemed to lose patience with her and, in a letter to his father, remarked that..

Aunt Franc evidently has a very unfortunate disposition.

Clearly, he was too young to understand what agonies she was experiencing, losing her husband and being in danger of losing the life she had come to love.

But it was typical of Franc that she found ways to stay busy and distract herself. One of her friends had written several pages of advice on how to get through her loneliness, including engaging in some sort of "uplifting work." Franc found the Associated Charities in Memphis and spent many hours there sorting clothes and listening to hard luck stories from the unemployed who came in daily. She wrote to Pat Bellingham in one of her frequent letters:

I have been trying to relieve some of the awful distress and suffering from actual hunger and cold - for which the poor were entirely unprepared.

Franc worked long days there, exhausting herself in her efforts to overcome her grief. But she was continually preoccupied with thoughts of Guatemala. She was worried about whether there were squatters at the Tameja *finca*. She wondered if Pat had seen any record of what Jekyll had been shipping. She asked about her boat, the *Lydia*, which she had rented out to the Anker Bros. and noted that it was the only income she had. She wondered if there was any buyer interested in Tameja or Los Angeles (the property on Lake Izabal). She wrote to Pat:

> *I wish I had back all the fruit and I would like nothing better than to ship it again or manage it. I cannot have one idea that I can settle myself in the U.S. to live the rest of my days. Horrible thought. I don't know what came over me yesterday, could not control my thoughts at all and my eyes burn from constant tears. I have not given up entirely, have been to church and the music was grand, on the finest organ in the south and this P.M. went for an auto spin over roads and with scenery that was all one could desire but such things only make me think of him more. Oh, Pat, it is so fierce, fierce, fierce. My sister and her family do everything possible to keep my mind occupied and to cheer me - but - oh, nothing helps or brings him back.*

Pat was clearly a kind and sympathetic man and he responded to her agonized epistles with as much reassurance as he could. He said that nothing had been abandoned into the hands of Jekyll and that he (Pat) could look at the Tameja books at any time. About the other questions she raised, he assured her that everything - the Los Angeles property, her warehouse in Livingston, the *Lydia* - was under control.

> *I am working my best for your interest and believe that all will yet come out fairly well. You will have to sacrifice part of the estate ... but keep up heart and I will do my best.*

But Franc was corresponding with others from Livingston. It is not clear who else she was hearing from - Lucy? BZ? Edward Reed? Doerscher? - but the stories she got from them fed her anger at Jekyll and Klanke and others whom she felt were treating her unfairly. When she complained to Pat, he reviewed the Tameja problems. The arbitration that was supposed to eliminate Klanke from any claim to ownership was being protested by him and was back in court. Since neither of the three - Franc, Jekyll or Klanke - could afford to buy the others out, Pat suggested she throw in her lot with Klanke rather than Jekyll. And he expressed his discouragement at her seeming dissatisfaction with him:

> *I would do anything for your husband or yourself. Hence it is more disheartening than I can tell you when, giving hours, days, and weeks in discussing your affairs with lawyers, etc. to hear that I am trying to do you out of what rightly belongs to you so that Klanke and I can get possession of the Tameja properties and work together ...It is all nonsense. ...I must confess that I have been wounded to the quick by the observations made by persons who have been in touch with you. We must work together...I am always at your disposition and will ever do my best for you so you need not get mad when you read this...*

We don't have her response to this but Franc must have apologized and in January, wrote a letter that was full of appreciation for all that Pat had done on her behalf. She was especially grateful that Sir Lionel Carden, the British Minister, had taken a stand for her and intended to protect her any way he could. She added:

> *I have been here nearly one year now and I don't feel any more like I can settle here than I did...nor do I have any clearer idea as to what I am to do or where to go. I just know that my heart and soul are there and I want to be brave enough to do something for myself somewhere there...I feel I have to go back very soon, if it is for only a short while, but you must all want to see me and be kind and loving to me to help me bear the first pangs.*

During the Memphis visit, there were, of course, lighter moments now and then. She took the children to the movies and went to see "Carmen" at the Opera house. In February, she and Bess had an Open House so that she could show off her curios from Guatemala. She hung sawfish and calabashes and arranged an appealing display. About sixty people came and seemed to enjoy it. The next day she wrote:

> *Spent the day repacking - didn't get half done - freezing cold in attic - sad job. Just one year ago these days I packed them in Guatemala and perspiration dripped over everything.*

She also worked on her clothes - always a favorite activity for Franc. After deciding to return south, she wrote:

> *I am going to sew every minute in the next few days, making up some linen goods I got in Belize nearly THREE years ago. Have not gotten one summer dress since I came and I am going to make FOUR dresses from the goods I got to make just one full skirt three years ago. How is that for economy, aided by the present skimpy fashions?*

How quickly the styles had changed - from full, floor-sweeping skirts with voluminous petticoats to the slimmer, uncorseted silhouette. Shirtwaists had come into fashion in America and could be worn with slightly shorter skirts - Walking Skirts or "Health Skirts." And Franc always kept up - her interest in clothes and fashion was lifelong. McCall and Butterick patterns had become available and sewing still seemed to give her pleasure. She could stitch away for hours, wherever she was, and often made things for others. While in Memphis she made dresses for Bess and for Aunt Lyda Strode who came for a visit, as well as a hat for Gladys to wear to her Confirmation at Calvary Church.

Late in February, Franc's brother-in-law, Jeff Burgie became ill and was in and out of the hospital. The doctor ordered him to go south until the weather warmed up so he and Bess and their daughter Frances left for New Orleans in early March. Franc remained in Memphis and took care of the other children, nursing J.L. through mumps and entertaining them with movies and trips to the park.

But Franc was now more than ready to get back to Guatemala. Having finally decided to go, she was packed and ready when Jeff and Bess returned. She visited the hairdresser, bought a hat and was on the train to New Orleans by April 15. She wrote:

> *Sat up all night, talked with the men in the observation car until 1 AM. Arrived in N.O. at 7:30. Had breakfast with Gene (*her nephew*) at Grunewald. Found out while steaming down the Mississippi that my trunks were not on board - the checks had been put on the wrong trunks.*

We shall see that keeping up with her luggage was an ongoing issue for Franc. She left bags in train stations, on boats, in trains and in houses where she visited. Perhaps her comment on an encounter she had on the steamer to Guatemala suggests the reasons she was sometimes distracted.

> *Got to talking with the young newspaper man, W. Jefferson Davis, going down with Hewitt and, as usual for me, had a pleasant experience with him. After I had talked with him about 15 minutes, he said, "You know, I like you - why have we not met before?"*

An attractive man - flattering remarks - pleasant conversation - who wouldn't forget her trunks? And when Franc arrived at Puerto Barrios, there were Lucy and BZ and other friends to meet her. Home at last. Perhaps....

Chapter 16
STAYING ON - OR NOT?

Franc was to spend two years more in Guatemala - from April, 1912 to April, 1914 - in a vain effort to get clear title to the property she owned as Will's heir. She had no place of her own to live - the consul house in Livingston was no longer available to her and Jekyll was ensconced at Tameja - so she stayed with friends or in hotels. She continued to have intense spells of grief and was greatly worried about money. There were frequent bouts of malarial chills and fever. Although she enjoyed some happy times with friends, her life as an almost-penniless widow was far different than it had been as the wife of a vice-consul and plantation owner.

Lucy Potts and BZ, however, were endlessly supportive. Franc spent much of her time during this period at Jocolo, Lucy's home on Lake Izabal. Her friendship was a fixed point in Franc's sometimes chaotic life.

As for BZ, he and Franc seemed to continue where they had left off, Will's death and his wife, Lola, notwithstanding. While Franc was in the States, they had corresponded and at one point she asked him to return a photo she had given him. He answered:

> *You want me to send you back your little photo, the sweetest I ever saw! Well, I won't do it. Ya esta! I keep it because some days when I am very triste, I need a thing to cheer me up and that little photo is just a thing to do so.*

There are indications in her diaries that she felt guilty about BZ, especially after Will's death. But she had saved notes they wrote to each other and among her memorabilia is an envelope full of those which she could not bring herself to throw away. On it she had written:

> *If anyone finds these notes and reads them, I request they do not think harm - there was nothing wrong - just child's play.*

Perhaps... At any rate, they saw each other often during this period, especially when she was staying at the hotel in Livingston. She sometimes used BZ's office at Theimer's to work on her business affairs. She needed him as a supportive friend - but also was not quite ready to give him up as a lover. She continued to write about their...

> *... blissful evenings on the steps.*

Very soon after her return, Franc was invited to Guatemala City to visit the Bellinghams. There she enjoyed reconnecting with the Owens and Ormsbys and Haggards and other friends from the diplomatic corps. There were teas and dances and dinners but she was anxious to try to settle her affairs and soon returned to Livingston. There she went to look at the papers Klanke had presented to try to prove his partial ownership of Tameja. She wrote:

> *There is a humbug about them.*

She learned more about the status of her other assets and liabilities: a house she owned that was being used by the Martinez Club; a warehouse in Livingston; the *Lydia*, her fruit boat; and a plantation called Los Angeles on Lake Izabal, a property which Will had bought but had not developed. There was also a loan made by Will to a man named Villataro which had not been repaid. There were many visits to the judge in attempts to settle claims and counter claims by Jekyll and Klanke. Franc put an embargo on everything Jekyll had. Jekyll wanted Franc to sign some papers about Klanke's claims, which she refused to do. Jekyll got into a fight about depositions and was put in jail briefly.

Franc had learned the previous year that getting in to see the judge was anything but easy. He was in the office only half a day and his reasons for not being in read like a "banana republic" comedy routine.

On October 26, Franc wrote:

> *Could not see judge. He began the fiesta.*

On November 5:

> *Fiesta still on. Could not see judge.*

On April 28:

> *Could not see judge. He was "under the influence" and had a quarrel with his <u>esposa.</u>*

She finally managed a day in court where she signed a division of the Los Angeles property between herself and Klanke. In November she settled the Villataro loan:

> *I settled the old account of Villataro - judge accepting the principal as full payment and he returned his <u>escrito</u> titles. Thank God - for I had spent the last money I brought with me, paying my board today.*

She tried to sell the Martinez Club house, filing papers to lower the price, but without success. On January 16. 1913, she wrote:

> *Passed in third solicitation to appoint a day for the sale of the Martinez house. But the judge was not in - Went to Custom House and wrote out another certification of <u>heredera</u> but too late to pass in - couldn't get stamped paper.*

Finally, with the help of Edward Reed, the new vice-consul, she found a renter for the house for $10 a month - but it was considerably less than she had asked.

And the struggle for Tameja dragged on.

Jocolo, home of Lucy on Lake Izabal

The waiting called forth all the patience Frank could muster. Up the river at Jocolo, she sewed, cared for sick people and pursued her interest in natural history. As noted, she had become the "go to" person for hookworm treatment and at Jocolo, affected people came to her almost daily. Others came because of various injuries, some because of malarial fevers. Some were too ill to be helped. One woman came the day after Franc arrived at Jocolo but died the next day and had to be buried there. Franc wrote that she seemed to be "suffocating."

Franc's own malaria recurred periodically and although she remarked that she was suffering terribly, she never slowed down for long, kept up with her voluminous correspondence and continued whatever project she was working on. January 8 was her birthday and in 1913, she wrote that she was 44 and that she weighed 150.

> *Horrors! Five horrors!....I cried nearly all day and read WFB's last letters to me. It gave me a fierce attack of grief. ...Lucy and I went for a long walk in the PM. She made me a birthday cake and my long life and happiness was drunk at dinner with champagne. We played 500...then at 10 PM, we killed a possom that had killed 6 or 7 chickens.*

That day's entry, with its range of emotions and activity, is so very Franc. She had given in to her sadness at memories of Will and experienced all over again her grief and loss. But, typically resilient, she pulled herself together and released her feelings in activity. After her long walk, her pain had eased and at dinner, she could live in the moment, enjoying her birthday and appreciating Lucy's effort to make it a celebration with all the trimmings. The day ended on a very practical note - as it always must in that environment - killing a possum to protect their chickens.

Franc's fondness for and interest in animals has been mentioned in relation to her little zoos at San Francisco and Tameja. She was intensely curious about their behavior and, at Jocolo, she and Lucy decided to watch the process by which butterflies emerge. They placed some worms in a box in December and watched as, in January, one emerged a mottled grey moth and one became a butterfly. One of her unpublished manuscripts is a detailed observation of a snake trying to swallow a frog which was desperately trying to save itself by holding on to a bush. Another short piece, published in a San Francisco paper, described the behaviour of leaf-cutting ants.

Sometimes, in spite of it all, Franc just seemed to have fun. One day she wrote:

> *Lucy and I went for a paddle up the Perdonales River. We went in swimming in our "altogethers" and an Indian came paddling along. Such screaming and scrambling. Such sport!*

Addie Owens came to visit and one day she and Franc went swimming and bathed a monkey and put a dress on him.

As she waited for something to be decided in Livingston or the Capital, Franc sewed, making ruffles for Lucy's bed and covers for screens in the house. She often spent all day sewing. The house at Jocolo looks, in photos, like an idyllic place to wait it all out. It was two stories high, spacious, with wide porches on all sides and situated right on the banks of the broad, tranquil lake. But it was somewhat isolated and she was often alone - except for the servants. Fortunately, boats passed frequently, making the trip to and from Livingston.

Franc made that trip often, trying to keep an eye on her business issues. She saw BZ when she was in Livingston staying at the hotel, using his office for her writing, and joining him for cocktails in the evenings. During one of her spells of fever, he brought her roses. She wrote in her code:

We sat on the steps, hugged and kissed and spooned - in bliss.

But sometime in 1913, another name made a brief appearance in Franc's diary. A Mexican named Rodolpho began a flirtation with her. We don't know where she met him but she wrote that they had a *tete a tete* and he sang Mexican songs to her. He also said very sweet things and wanted to hug and kiss. She noted that it was a temptation - but one that, it appears, she was able to resist.

As for the property issue, it continued to fester with no remedy in sight. Franc noted that Jekyll had gotten into a fight when the court demanded proof of his entitlement to Tameja and had spent a night in Jail. He was still fighting with Klanke over his demands for a share of it all. In Feburary, 1913. Franc managed to see the judge to get an embargo and deposition fixed up. She returned to Jocolo and soon received a visit by a "delegation." She described it ironically in her diary:

> *Jekyll came up bringing his power of attorney. And George Ferguson with his law books and numerous <u>escritos</u>, and the Alcalde of San Felipe, Juan Guiterrez, with his cane of office and his pen and ink, and a policeman with his billy. I was in bed with a fever but got up and found out what it was all about. They said I must be in Livingston on the second, which will be Sunday. I must show my inventories and either stay in town or have a power of attorney. There is no way to get in town for a week. I signed nothing.*

On March 7, as Franc continued to suffer with fever, Lucy went to Livingston to try to deal with the issues but came back, saying that she could do nothing.

Franc's correspondence with Pat Bellingham continued and in March, he assured her that he had been working on her behalf and had accomplished several things at the *Registro* in Zacapa. She was legally recognized as Will's heir and protected in regard to her share in the various properties - but the claims and counter-claims of Jekyll and Klanke continued and he advised her to settle somehow with Jekyll:

> *As long as you keep digging at him, I take it he will keep digging at you and so goes the merry game until the Bank swoops down one day and puts your half of the property up for auction.*

Franc learned, when finally seeing the judge in May, that her embargos on Jekyll had been raised. Edward Reed went with her for another visit to him but that, too, was a disappointment and she wrote:

> *I can do nothing more, or it is not worthwhile - so that is finished.*

Was it? Did Franc pack her bags and leave on the next steamer out? Not quite! There had to be a final visit to Guatemala City to say farewell to the Bellinghams and Haggards and Owens and other friends. She was there for two months playing bridge, going to "at homes" and parties and dances, sewing for herself and others - and managing to do one last thing to disturb society there. She was invited to the home of a man she had met and liked - Mr. Anderson, a Finn. She wrote that:

> *It was a regular bohemian affair - 5 men and 2 ladies.*

A bit later, he became ill and she - never able to resist a sick person in need - spent a good deal of time caring for him. She seems not to have realized - or perhaps thought it unimportant - that, at that time, a single woman visiting a single man - even a very sick one - in his rooms was not the done thing. Lucy later enlightened her.

> *Mrs. Potts told me the people in Guatemala City searingly criticized me and said awful things about me and ostracized me because I took care of the dying Finn.*

While in the City, Franc did make a little progress with her financial affairs. She was able to pay off a debt she owed on the Los Angeles property and turned over some shares to the Banco Americano.

At the end of July, Franc was ready to return to Livingston. Her arrival there was, in a sense, the beginning of the end, an almost desperate finale to her Guatemala life. As she began to pack, she was warmly supported by her good friends - Lucy, BZ, the Bellinghams - but a new name began to appear in her diary in August. Felix Tripeloury was a young German - 25 or so - who appeared in Livingston that summer. She wrote:

> *We became friends at once. He kissed my hands...the first night. We remembered each other from the time he went up to Coban 3 or 4 months ago....A dear sweet German, a Dr. of Law, highly educated - I have learned so much about many things from him..*

Their friendship continued for many years, perhaps until her death. She often mentioned in her diaries receiving letters from "darling Felix." In her final days in Guatemala, he tried to help straighten out her legal problems, even making a vain trip to Guatemala City.

Final Days

Franc began packing up all her possessions - her diary is full of lists. But suddenly, in August, she seems to be harvesting bananas at Tameja! While in Guatemala City, Franc had gotten a letter from Lucy telling her that Jekyll had gone to the States. It was her chance to go to the *finca* at last. She began to hire workers and took them with her to Tameja. On August 11, she wrote,

> *Left Livingston at 9:30 AM with <u>Signet</u> towing 3 pitpains and 4 men and 3 women - a fruit crew..*

Felix Tripeloury went with her and they accompanied the crew out into the bush at the far end of the plantation, stopping at the Guatemala House camp and at Coolie Hill. The diary is full of hash marks counting the bunches that were cut. Franc noted that she paid three men and three women $278 for three days but the frantic harvesting went on for two-three weeks. Then, on August 29, she wrote at Tameja:

> *Hombre Gordo* (pilot on one of the river boats) *passed up early and said Jekyll was in town and was coming up. He said he would pass down about 3 to take me down. I don't know what I will do.*

What she did was return to Livingston and fight on, though it seemed hopeless. Again Franc spent some time at Jocolo, sewing, sometimes enjoying the peace and quiet of the place and, in September, remembering the anniversary of Will's death.

> *After dinner, I went down on the wharf alone and let out the tears that were bursting my heart. I felt a little relieved.*

It was a trying time as she traveled back and forth, up and down the river. Felix Tripeloury was in Guatemala City trying to make some headway with her problems but she was hearing nothing from him at first. She wrote on September 26:

> *I am wildly nervous and <u>triste</u>...and wondering how I am doing to endure.*

On October 9, they celebrated Lucy's 71st birthday and Franc wrote that there was a severe earthquake at 12:30. Then Franc had another attack of fever. And it rained constantly, coming down in torrents, that tropical rain like sheets of water. She wrote to Felix almost daily and began to get frequent letters from him. She was alone at Jocolo much of the time except for occasional visitors and helped to paint a room.

Finally, in late October, the rains stopped and the sun came out and on November 7, Franc learned that Jekyll had left Guatemala permanently for the States. She went down immediately to Livingston and made plans to go to Tameja. Then she learned that Villatoro had the key to the house there. She demanded that he give it to her. He would not. She wrote:

> *I gave him a piece of my mind and told him I was going to Tameja without the keys - when I was ready.*

But she did not go immediately, noting that she was not well enough. A little later, she visited Villatoro again but found him the same. She went then to visit a lawyer, Moreno, who told her that Villatoro had a power of attorney from Jekyll and could have her put in jail if she went to Tameja. Her next step was to visit the judge who told her that she must get possession of her rights in the courts. In the meantime,

> *All the Villatoro tribe got off, to live at Tameja. 18 all told. 7 grown-ups, 11 children.*

In a letter to Pat that day, she expressed her rage and despair over this desecration of her home.

> *I had <u>to calmly witness the occupation of my little home</u> by a motley, dirty, ragged band of natives and Indians. All to roam at will in and about my little home that still contains <u>many evidences of my home touch as to comfort and ornamentation - also personal articles.</u> Oh, God, that is heaping insult upon injury! While I have to roam up and down with "nowhere to lay my head."*

Still, Franc was not ready to give up and go. She believed that she had all the documentation needed to prove her case and listed it in her diary: Will's will signed and witnessed on December, 1905; a signed and witnessed statement that she was the legitimate and only heir of W. Forrester Brown, October 1, 1910; titles and maps of Los Angeles; certificate from the land office of Los Angeles with division of property between her and Klanke. During December she remained in Livingston at a house on Hill Street, visiting BZ often and continuing to use his office to write.

Of course, Franc continued to express her anger, frustration and despair to Pat in frequent letters. Finally, he wrote her in December that, in his opinion, she should have the undisputed right to go to Tameja and work the plantation as long as she gave Villatoro, as Jekyll's representative, half the proceeds. But the endlessly patient Pat was clearly becoming weary of the amount of time required to try to straighten out her affairs. He told her that he was at the beck and call of the supervisor at the British legation and had a new minister to deal with. Much as he wanted to help, he wrote:

> *I literally have not the time to see to your matters, which as a matter of fact, <u>would fully employ a lawyer all the time.</u>*

Franc spent Christmas of 1913 at Jocolo, writing all day, and on January 8, she celebrated her 44th birthday there. She wrote:

> *Weigh 150 lb. Sewed all day - no one knew it was my birthday.*

Where was Lucy?

On January 10, 1914, Franc tried again to see the judge, presenting her *escrito* dated December 23. She tried again on the 17th but he had gone to Port and did not return. So she followed him and came back on the boat with him, talking with him there. But she wrote:

> *I don't think he is going to do much.*

Franc went again to see him on the 19th - but he told her that her inventories have never been proven. After seeing him, she wrote in her diary:

> *I don't understand things.*

Franc was, of course, being robbed. As a woman at that time, she had few property rights even in the more civilized parts of the world. In America, one quarter of the states at that time denied a wife the right to own property; one third of them allowed her no claim on her own earnings. In Guatemala, these difficulties were multiplied. It hardly mattered what her legal claims were, how capable of running the business she might be, how strong a personality she had, how many friends she had. Perhaps she was seen as stubborn and difficult to deal with - but would a little more charm and sweetness have helped? Only if she had had a well-connected male "protector" whom she could dazzle with feminine wiles and manipulate behind the scenes.

Franc wrote a furious letter full of conflicting emotions to Pat.

> *I found through a long conversation with the lawyer that Jekyll did leave a power of attorney with Villatoro. I just want to see the judge to find out if they would take me with police force and put me in jail if I went to Tameja...If he tells me that he would not go to that extreme, I will sure go and perhaps even brave that extreme for I don't care what happens to me. I am sick and am ready for anything, it is preferable to my present miserable existence.*
>
> *I don't want to tie myself to Tameja permanently for I don't want to be bound to anything. I prefer freedom to anything else, even at the expense of pure poverty but what hurts is the awful injustice and unfairness and the low-down-ness of it all. It gives me the chills and fever just to think there are such creatures in the world and there is not a soul in this country to even speak a word in my favor. Don't tell me anything about what ministers and consuls are here for.*
> *It is such injustice that drives women to be militant suffragists and joy be with them and it is what makes men-haters and let us hope that women will have courage to do even worse than they do. The world started out wrong is the trouble and I would go to any extreme to help women put it right.*
> *...the easiest way out of it all is to go to Tameja and resist arrest..*
> *Please get my affairs fixed up with all dispatch (but what is the use of asking you) so that things will not be too much of a muddle when "something drops."*

The letter must have scorched Pat's fingers. But with his usual patience and calm, he continued to handle her affairs as best he could. In February, 1914, he finished arranging the division of Los Angeles and contacted a lawyer to assure that she had a clean title to her half of it. That would turn out to be the only asset she had to pass on to nieces and nephews at her death.

On January 24, Franc went to see the judge, taking Edward Reed with her.

> *We had a talk and I understand what further monkey business he wants me to do.*

Reed tried to help but was no more successful than Franc in his efforts to see the judge. On January 26, Franc wrote:

> *He has a nephew here and so was running around with him. Said he would come in the PM but in the PM, he went up river with a black gang of public street women.*

Again, in February, Franc got her papers together to present. On March 2, she gave Reed $50 to get a stamped paper in Port to copy a last thing for the court. But on the 14th, she wrote:

> *Could do nothing in court. Give up.*

This time, Franc did.

PART 2

Chapter 17

FAREWELL TO THE TROPICS

Franc did not write about her final days in Guatemala but they must have been painful in the extreme. She had been packing and preparing for several months and had decided that her first destination would be Ireland. Will's family had been urging her to come ever since Will's death four years earlier. Perhaps also she was postponing the day when she would have to go home to her own family and rely on them for financial support. As far as I have been able to determine, she never returned to Guatemala although she continued to correspond regularly with friends she had made there - with some until the end of her life.

Franc sailed from New York on the ship *Amerika* in May, 1914. There, to see her off, was her nephew, Hudson Strode, and an old Monticello friend, Hat McKeller. She noted in her diary that BZ was on board the ship, along with her friend, Pablo Doerscher. In a post card to her nephew, Howard, she wrote:

> *Six days out and all's well. Perfect weather, splendid ship. Just like some big, beautiful hotel by the sea. Had one dance but nothing I ever saw danced before. Fine music with the very good meals. My two German friends are on board and are nice to me. We three sit together at meals, a small table for three. I take walks on deck - 4 times around is a mile.*

One wonders if BZ and Pablo deliberately planned their trip to Europe to accompany Franc and look out for her welfare. She says no more about them after the arrival in England and probably they went on to Germany to visit family and friends. Though Franc and BZ corresponded occasionally for several years, this seems to be the last time they were together. It is hard not to speculate about the romantic possibilities on board a grand ocean liner - but she is silent on that and there are no remarks about blissful evenings on deck. Perhaps Doerscher's presence was inhibiting. Overall, as she embarked on this voyage, Franc seemed ready to try to put the past behind her - and perhaps that included BZ as a lover.

When Franc landed at Southhampton on May 31, 1914, she could not have anticipated the momentous events that would happen on British soil within the next two months. She was met by Mrs. Spencer and spent a month in London before going to Ireland. The Anglo-American Exposition was in progress so she visited that and saw several other friends from Guatemala days. One was Rowland Ormsby whom we will hear much more about during her New York years. She wrote:

> *Went to lunch and crickett with Rowland. Then to his flat where I stayed to dinner and spent the evening - with Mrs. Ormsby - the 2nd. The first is still living.*

Franc was moved to return to her room and write a long letter to "the first" back in Belize. In London, she seemed to be determined to enjoy herself and put her recent painful experiences behind her. She commented on going to the Hippodrome to a play and to the Army and Navy Club where, she noted, "ladies smoke." In Hyde Park, she,

> *.....saw and heard strange things. I saw more people in a minute that I had seen in 10 years together.*

Always concerned about her appearance, she visited a hair dresser and decided to have her hair dyed black - but then noted:

> *It is not a success, yet.*

On July 15, Franc traveled to County Cashel to visit Will's family. They greeted her with open arms and the first few days were full of social events - garden party after garden party, some very grand, and a flower show on a large estate. But then, on August 3, she wrote:

> *Germany declared war on Russia which involves <u>all Europe</u>.... England had to declare war against Germany. France, also.....*

Thus began the "War to End All Wars", and in short order, all of Europe was plunged into it. Franc noted that all social engagements and tennis games had been called off, then remarked,

> *The "volunteers" now <u>supposed</u> to be ready to fight for England in their common danger marched up to the house and drilled a little. It was very dark. They were collecting and the girls gave them something and they gave three cheers for the Misses Brown. One of the head men said they would defend the coast of Ireland in case of being attacked by an enemy - but will not leave Ireland to fight for England.*

Franc seemed to take a rather dim view of their enthusiasm for the cause - which turned out to be prescient when Ireland, after cooperating enthusiastically at the beginning of the war, objected strongly to the possibility of conscription in 1918.

Franc had one of her attacks of fever in August but with her usual energy, she attended the first meeting of the First Aid group. She continued with this and in October, passed third in the exams. She also spent many days sewing for the soldiers, sometimes in "sewing bees" with other girls and women. Often she directed these. Some days in her diary she wrote only:

> *Sewing for soldiers and wounded.*

Throughout September and October this war work continued. But there were other, more leisurely activities, such as trying to ride a bicycle ("I smashed my shin"), gathering mushrooms, playing tennis, going for long walks, and playing golf for the first time.

While in Ireland, Franc wrote that she attended church quite frequently. She went not only to the Anglican Cathedral but also to Chapel (Methodist). Most Sundays, she went to one in the morning and the other in the afternoon or evening. Later in her life, she made other religious choices, becoming a Christian Scientist and dabbling heavily, for a time, in Spiritualism, attending seances and visiting psychics. She never wrote about the thoughts and feelings that motivated these choices. Clearly, she was looking for "answers" after her very painful experiences of the last few years. She had to find a way to live her changed life - life as a woman on her own without much money to smooth the way. Far from being the rich aunt we envisioned later, she was entering a period of financial uncertainty that would last for much of her life.

As Fall set in, Franc noted that the weather had become fierce, and her mood, seemingly, with it:

> *A fearful day - strong wind - pelting rain - and cold. I did not put my nose out the door. Sewed. Did odd jobs. Wrote to Mrs. Bellingham. Am too nervous and worried for words. Can't get a word from Mrs. B and she right here at Butterant - not two hours from here.*

Franc's old correspondent, Pat, recipient of her anguished letters in Guatemala, seemed to be nearby with his wife, visiting their family home in Ireland. Franc must have worried that she had antagonized them beyond forgiveness - but finally, she heard from them. That helped her mood - but she continued to have days when she felt worried and *triste*. There were also hints of family problems. She wrote in her code that John..

> *....drank whole bottle in a few hours.*

And when Franc bought a bottle for herself, Lil drank all but two drinks from it. She wrote:

> *I am miserably nervous and sad.*

Then Effie had a recurrence of psychiatric problems and Franc took her to a hospital for the mentally ill where, it seems, she had been before.

With these family tensions, the war raging and some physical problems which Franc wrote about in her code (in this case, unreadable), she was ready to get home to America. In August, she wrote to the Richard Bulman agency and asked for a list of steamship departures. An interesting exchange of letters followed between Franc and Douglas Bulman - evidently a friend as well as her agent. There were some differences of opinion about the War and the Germans, in particular. He wrote to her in November:

> *The papers I sent you were only intended to convey that perhaps the U.S.A. may not see eye to eye with us in our present undertaking! And I have heard it expressed that the States would like to see us humbled....So when you return across the seas, do put your friends right.*

He went on to say how much he wished he could be fighting but was prevented by asthma and chest problems. Airing his feelings about the Germans, he wrote:

> *I always disliked them and they have proved by their disgraceful conduct that my opinion was about right...My sister who was in the States last year said heaps of Americans openly boast of their German blood. And all the world knows the large number of Germans who are citizens of the U.S.A. But you take it from me that with the hostility they have been showing lately, the only places they will be welcome will be Germany and Austria - if they exist! I don't think you have any idea of the bitterness that any friends of Germany will experience...that is why I am writing you at such length.*

Douglas wrote Franc again in December just before she was to leave. This time he was responding to a question she had asked him about using her American passport. He said that she must not do that as she was a British subject by marriage and she would be guilty of fraud and subject to a heavy fine or imprisonment! He added:

> *What's the matter with Great Britain that you want to strike her colours?*

In a postscript, he couldn't resist another dig at the Germans.

> *We English people are not like Germans who treat official papers as scraps of paper; and you will forgive me if I say I am surprised at your proposal re the passport.*

We don't have Franc's side of this correspondence. She probably wanted to use an American passport because America was not yet in the War and she felt it would somehow make her passage smoother. But whatever she said about the war, she clearly had not expressed sufficient hostility to Germany to suit this very patriotic Brit. She had had many German friends in Guatemala - including her dear BZ; perhaps she could not believe they were as bad as all that.

At any rate, she booked her passage for December 21. But before leaving the country, she finally received a note from Pat Bellingham who was in Ireland still and apologized for not seeing her. He told her the situation with Tameja was still a mess and Jekyll was in the states, paying little attention. He said that Franc's papers were in a safe deposit box at Banco Americano but that there was no one now in Guatemala who was looking after her affairs. He promised to put together an accounting soon.

With this news in mind, Franc left Dublin on December 21, 1914. She sailed from Liverpool on the *SS Arabica*. The ship was crowded with soldiers but she wrote that, thanks to Douglas,

> *I got a fine big room on the promenade deck...a motley crowd of passengers from 8 or 9 nations.*

And right away she met a congenial man - a German who, she said,

> *...is often mistaken for the Crown Prince.*

For Christmas Day, a collection was taken up to give the children on the ship a treat and there was a party for them in the 3rd class dining room. On December 26, she wrote that the weather was very bad and the seas were high but she and the German had a cigarette on deck. On the following day she noted that the weather was still ferocious but she was getting around and making some new acquaintances.

The high winds continued amid snow squalls and lasted for most of the remaining days of the trip. Many, including the crew, were seasick. But Franc was not and continued to enjoy the company of the handsome Crown Prince look-alike. She wrote:

I am having a sweet time with my German.

And that continued until they reached New York on January 3 and parted with kisses and hugs. Of course, Douglas would have been appalled but, presumably, Franc was wise enough not to write him about it.

As they arrived in New York harbor in the early morning, Franc pronounced the sunrise "wonderful" and seemed happy to be back in the States. She was met by two of the Susans, Hat McKeller and Lil Lamm, and spent the next three months in and around the city. It seemed to be a time for pleasure and for re-connecting with old friends - although the question of where she would eventually settle and how she would manage financially was undoubtedly always on Franc's mind. She and Hat and others went to the theater, visited a variety of churches, dined out, went to the zoo, played cards, went for drives and attended meetings of the "Monticello girls."

At one of the dinners, Franc met a man named Jess with whom the carried on a flirtation for several weeks and enjoyed kisses and blissful evenings. There is no doubt that Franc liked men and was not shy about indulging in the physical pleasures of their company. She always wrote about that in her code, some of which is hard to decipher - but "bliss" and "kiss" can always be translated. We can leave the rest to the imagination, bearing in mind that it was - perhaps - a more inhibited time. Certainly, it was a more reticent one.

In February, Franc made a trip to Philadelphia where she met her old friend, archaeologist George Byron Gordon, at the University of Pennsylvania Museum. It had been 12 years since she was his hostess in Guatemala and visited with him the ruins at Quirigua but they had corresponded regularly. She wrote:

> *We dined together and sat at the table til nearly 1 o'clock. Had*
> *a great talk over old times and life in general.*

From Philadelphia, Franc traveled on to Washington where she was met by other friends from Guatemala days and spent a week experiencing the unique pleasures that city offers and meeting some of its important people. She visited the Corcoran Gallery, the Senate, St. Paul's Church, and the D.A.R. building. Lots of names were dropped - there were congressmen and senators, an ex-secretary of war, a Canadian portrait artist, and a "well known writer." Some family members later referred to Franc as bit of a "snob" and these diary entries might give that impression. But to see her in that light, one would have to forget about her Guatemalan train rides in cattle cars with inebriated workers or her relentless tramps around New York looking for humble filing jobs or her cold, anxious nights with morphine addicted patients.

Back in New York, she was happy to be able to see the Owens family again, especially her friend, Addie. They were passing through and Addie was quite ill. Franc "doctored" her and was soon able to see her and her sisters off on the SS Philadelphia.

At this point, Franc had to give serious thought to how she would live, financially. She had left Guatemala owning half of the Los Angeles *finca*, Klanke owning the other half - but it was not under cultivation. She also seems to have had some Banco Americano stock or bonds which yielded a very small income from time to time. But that was all - she must either find work - or go to her family for help.

So as February came to a close, Franc began to note in her diary what looked like some job overtures on her part. She went to a free employment bureau and wrote to the Rockefeller Sanitary Commission about her work with hookworm. But a few days later, she decided it was time to leave New York for Miami where job prospects seemed brighter. It is not clear just what motivated this move. Lucy Potts had a home there where Franc would stay from time to time. This time Lucy was not there - but possible jobs were.

Chapter 18
NURSING ADDICTS IN MIAMI

Franc sailed from New York to Miami on March 10, 1915, on the SS Mallory. The ship was full of soldiers who were headed for the Mexican border. She noted rather unhappily that she had to have a roommate - but ultimately, found her "rather interesting." The voyage was short and she arrived in Miami on the 13th.

It is hard to tell where Franc was staying - though eventually, she was with Lucy. For the first few weeks there, she wrote very little in her diary except to note the people she was corresponding with. She was a prodigious letter-writer - to family (Bess, Sis, Aunt Lyda, Will's sister Lil) Guatemala friends - Lucy, Addie, Gordon, Tripiloury, Agatha, Bellingham. During this time, she seemed to spend several hours every day at her correspondence. She also attended Woman's Club meetings and church and mentioned meetings of the Equal Franchise League and the Women's Christian Temperance Union. Going to meetings and participating in organizations and clubs was the done thing for emancipated women at that time. Certainly, it was a way of meeting new people and becoming a part of the community. All along, though, Franc mentioned that she was writing to various doctors about her experience in treating hookworm. She went to meet with a Dr. Brunner - but then wrote "nothing doing."

However, finally, on April 20, Franc wrote:

> _Red Letter Day_ - _began treatment at 4:30 for dope habit, a young woman about 30...Miami, Florida....under supervision of Dr. Brunner._

This was the first of several patients Franc worked with in Miami who were undergoing withdrawal from morphine. She was excited about this first patient because it was a real job where she could make some money of her own and not have to be dependent on friends and family. All those years of working with sick and injured patients in

149

Guatemala had given her the confidence to sell herself as a sort of "practical nurse" even though she had no formal training. She was able to make her living working with similar patients for the next couple of years. It was exhausting work, often in squalid circumstances - but perhaps she relished the difficulties as a distraction from her own pain and her worries about her future. And, as we have seen, she genuinely sympathized with what her patients were enduring.

The treatment for morphine addiction at that time consisted of giving the patients scopolamine over a period of 2-3 days, in which the patients would become delirious. They suffered extreme anxiety and could become wildly agitated. Often they became disoriented and experienced hallucinations. It was important for a caregiver to be there to administer the proper dosages at designated times and to be on the watch when the delirium took hold. Franc wrote of this first patient:

...began the "Twilight Sleep" about 9:30 AM. ... I am on the watch every moment. She was not still 15 seconds to take her pulse.

But she continued giving the doses and two days later wrote that the patient was coming out of the "sleep" and does not want the drug. Franc was paid for a week's work and began to contact other doctors in hopes of finding more patients. However, this effort was interrupted when she began to receive letters and cables from her sister, Bess, that Jeff Burgie was very ill. Franc realized that she was needed and left Miami for Memphis on May 9.

Jeff Burgie's Death

Franc's diaries for the next two months deal primarily with Jeff's final illness. He was suffering from a serious, life-threatening heart condition although the details are not clear. Having had much experience with sickness, she was able to discuss his treatment with the two doctors involved - who didn't seem to agree or consult with each other. Jeff rallied for a time in June but then deteriorated. Franc wrote that -

His stomach turned against all medicine.

And, to add to the family's anxieties, Frances, the youngest daughter of Bess and Jeff, became ill with a fever and a trained nurse had to come in to stay with her. On June 20, Bess's older sister Sallie (Sis) came from Kentucky to be with them. And on July 13, 1915, Jeff died. Franc wrote:

> *JLB passed on at twelve forty-five. Something awful - poor Bess is very bad and the children also.*

Within a couple of weeks, the family - Bess, J.L. Jr, Gladys and Frances - left in a touring car and Franc was alone. She supervised the cleaning of the house and prepared it for the family's return but then she herself was able to enjoy a respite at a resort in Tennessee and to visit with her Martin relatives (her mother's family). Gibson Wells was the site of a healing spring near Trenton. Franc's description of the trip there, accompanied by her nephew, Charlie, sounds like a page from her Guatemala diaries rather than a jaunt in the civilized USA. They took a train, then changed to a car but the roads were so bad, they had to get out and walk through mud several times and spend the night in a farm house.

When Franc got there, she stayed for two weeks. It is hard to know who was with her, although she mentioned "Aunt J" a couple of times. On the 14th, she wrote:

> *Same program every day - walk to well to get water - eat three big meals a day -and sleep.*

On the 16th:

> *Lo mismo.*

On the 18th:

> *Lo mismo. Played bridge some. Began raining.*

After two weeks there, she returned to Memphis but was soon off to visit the Swifts whom she had known in Guatemala. Their home in Georgia was called Bonnie Oaks and Franc was to visit them several times. While there, she enjoyed horseback riding and fishing. When she got back to Memphis, there was a letter from Lucy who was in Miami and longing for a visit from her dear friend, Franc. Franc noted that she hated leaving Bess - but on October 6, she did.

Miami

For the next year and a half, Franc was able to find enough work in Miami to support herself as she was so eager to do. It was all very well to make visits to relatives at healing springs or to fish with friends at their plantations - but these were not a solution to the problem of how she would live her life as a single woman. So the morning after she got to Miami, she rose early and visited a doctor she knew. He had nothing for her but the very next day she got a call from a surgeon named Jones who sent her to a patient who was taking the cure for morphine addiction. She was with him constantly for four days, administering the doses of scopolamine, watching for his reaction, trying to calm him as he withdrew from the drug - and earning $20.

That patient seems easy compared to some who came later but even so, Franc noted that she got almost no rest and had to lie down on the floor to try to sleep. These jobs were not only exhausting but took place often in physically unpleasant conditions. But without formal training, she found them the easiest to get. She described several of these experiences with morphine addicts in her diary.

There was Mr and Mrs. Webb, both addicted but with no money. Franc took them on anyway - *por nada* - and put them under scopolamine in turn. Their actions alternated between quiet and wild and she got no rest day or night. She stayed with them for seven days until she was sure they were getting on well enough. When she left, they were a little shaky and nervous still and she herself was exhausted, having earned not a cent of pay. Unfortunately, Mrs. Webb relapsed and several months later, Franc wrote:

> *Took the Webb woman again - at Miss Lizzie's - too <u>horrible for words.</u> Don't believe she will ever give up morphine - the woman is <u>fierce</u> - has been like a cyclone every minute.*

Franc spent Thanksgiving staying with a male patient in rooms the doctor had engaged. She was with him for 10 days and it was a painful struggle:

> *Patient restless in the night, begged for morphine - but I had none.*

In February, she stayed with a patient who was a charity case. In March she wrote:

> *Came out to Hardyville to a house called "September Morn" - House of Ill Fame - to give Ruby Davis she morphine cure. Began scopolomine at 9:20 AM.*

The following day Franc wrote:

> *Girl getting on but giving a lot of trouble. She phoned a Dr. Stuart to meet her in a certain house. I followed her and met Dr. S and told him what I was doing.*
>
> *Had quite a "discussion" - Finally got the girl back to the house. Today she was a little better.*

But the next day, Franc left there - in a car the patient ordered. Franc asked her for $20 - but got only $10.

There were other patients throughout the year, all lasting one to two weeks, some paying, some not. In September, 1916, Dr. Brenner asked her to take on 2 morphine patients in the same house - a man and a woman. Franc noted that she agreed, though there was no money in sight, and wrote about it at some length.

On the 24th, she wrote

> *Kelly apparently all right. Put Irene under at 9 AM.*
> *Irene was very bad all night. Tore off her nightgown and tore up the bedspread. It was a terrible nightmare of a night. Mrs. Anderson came...she saw the full effect of the drug on the girl. She watched for an hour while I curled up on a little child's bed and*

slept. Had been awake 3 nights. No rest in the day. Kelly began to complain and act queer. Finally complained so much of terrible pains and all symptoms of lack of morphine - he finally confessed to having taken it during the scopolamine - given to him by Irene while I was out of the room. So that accounted for his non-delirium. I was heartbroken. I shed tears when it was necessary to give him morphine again. It was <u>cruel - a crime.</u> Gave him codeine through the day but he had to have more morphine that night.

On the 26th,

Irene came through alright but had a terrible night. Had to send for the Dr. at 3 AM. She was in a terrible state, in contortions, and I was <u>frightened.</u> She got better and apparently getting on as usual - like the bad ones. Began elimination capsules with Kelly again at 2 PM. Had to watch and work with Irene all day. Mrs. A did not come back. I bathed the little boy here, had him say his prayers and put him to bed. Have to keep the whole house clean. The man does the cooking. When I could get an hour's sleep, I occupied half the dining table, the dishes on the other half. No cot or anything for me to stretch out on when there's a chance. The house is very clean but the out of door closet is <u>awful</u> - too awful for words. The mosquitoes have been fierce. House is screened but they <u>will</u> keep the doors open. Two sisters or half sisters of Irene say they are her father's daughters by a third wife. One runs an establishment in Hardyville. One of them has promised to pay me. One, I believe, is the mother of the darling little boy - he does not know who his parents are.

Not all Franc's patients that year were addicts, of course. But the work took its toll. Of her visit to a new patient in March, 1917, she wrote:

Have had all kinds of experiences over the week. They were going to have me have tuberculosis - because I cleared my throat a few times. And because my darling passed on 6 1/2 years ago - the doctor said it must have been TB. And because I was looking dilapidated and weary and worn when I came out here. I was ready to leave them - but then they begged me to remain - so I did - I need the money and the change so badly.

Of course, it was not all work and no play and from time to time, Franc enjoyed a few flirtations. She took some of them quite seriously. Given her passionate nature, she fell hard and then suffered agonies of anxiety when the man of the moment seemed to lose interest. In Miami, his name was Carlos and he was "too sweet for words." For a few days, they were like sweethearts. Then he began to ignore her and she wrote

I nearly had a hysterical spell about it. I must stop thinking of him.

Apparently, she did - and after a few days, ceased to mention him. But this pattern repeated itself off and on as the years of Franc's widowhood continued. She seemed genuinely to suffer for a time - but then she was able to let it go. It does not seem to have been in her character to pine away, longing for the unattainable. She was, perhaps, too practical and had too much energy. Over time, she developed a thicker skin and a more skeptical view of male protestations of devotion.

When not working at nursing jobs, Franc tried making a living in Miami in other ways. She began to write up some of her Guatemalan experiences and send them to various publications. She mentioned American Magazine, National Geographic, Catholic World, Harpers Monthly, and American Lumberman. Most were returned rejected but the latter took her article about mahogany harvesting and paid her $3.00. Otherwise, she kept busy at the Business Women's League and at church activities and social events.

In March of 1917, Franc wrote that she was looking for a room to rent; apparently, Lucy had left the city. She was finding nothing that she could afford and money was an increasing problem. She wrote one day after a visit to the bank,

Could do nothing but write to Bess.

And Bess, as always, came through, sending her a wire urging her to return to Memphis at once. Franc did, noting that there were..

..no interesting people on the train - old folks and such like.

No Crown Prince look-alikes, no interesting newspapermen, no Latin lovers. But she settled in to the Burgie home for a time - with Bess and the three teenagers - and began to look for work while also being active, as usual, in clubs and charities and church.

During this period in 1917, Franc mentioned attending the Christian Science Church and it remained her religious choice for years to come - perhaps until the end of her life. Founded by Mary Baker Eddy, it was the fastest growing religion in America in the first decades of the 20th century. It was one of several metaphysical religions that emerged during this period. Its followers believe that the spirit world is central and the mind is the key to physical health. Therefore, there was no need for doctors and hospitals and medicines. A Christian Science practitioner's job was, through prayer and attention to the reading of Mrs. Eddy's *Science and Health,* to persuade the patient that he/she is not ill and will recover. There was no need for laying on of hands or other tactile forms of healing practice. One could "heal" this way even on the phone.

Franc did not write anything to let us know what attracted her to Christian Science. The spiritual dimension was clearly important for her and led her on to explore other, more radical forms of spiritualism, including seances and manifestations of life beyond the grave. It must have led also to her attendance at classes and lectures on Eastern religions of various kinds. She was looking for answers as she determined to live her life as a free and independent woman.

Chapter 19
NURSING IN MEMPHIS

As the summer of 1917 began, Franc made a visit that she would eventually repeat yearly. She traveled to the farm near Columbus, Kentucky where her sister, Sallie, and husband Charles Pennebaker, lived, along with their daughter Ruth, a young lady of about 20. One might expect a quiet, restful time - but Franc threw herself into farm work with much the same energy she had exhibited in her activities in Memphis, Miami and Guatemala. She helped Ruth throw a party, went to Red Cross meetings, and was constantly busy with household chores. She washed, mended, scrubbed floors, enameled a tub, pulled grass, sewed. She wrote,

> *Nearly finished yard. Have done absolutely nothing else - nor thought of anything else - and am too tired and achey to rest at night.*

When Franc was involved in a project - whether sorting clothes at a charity, cleaning house, weeding the garden or making a dress - she drove herself hard, sometimes to exhaustion. She wrote in July of 1917 that she felt pretty ill but..

> *...worse when I am not at something.*

Entertainment in Columbus consisted of going in to town to a "Womanless Wedding" and helping niece Ruth give a Rook Party for her friends. Franc commented, wryly,

> *All the youth and beauty of Columbus were here - we gave pineapple ice and cake.*

On her return to Memphis in August, Franc was happy to get a new set of lessons from F.S.C.D. This seems to have been a school which offered correspondence courses in filing, shorthand and related office skills. During a lengthy visit with the Swifts in Georgia, she worked on these lessons along with writing some articles, going to card parties and attending Red Cross meetings. There was also some "sightseeing" that included a visit to a dairy farm. Even after all her travels and her varied experiences, she could still be impressed and amused by a 2100 pound bull and an 800 pound cow!

Back in Memphis, Franc began her last few months of living with the Burgies - and took on her last few jobs as a nurse. She also made a new friend whose companionship enriched her life there and endured through correspondence for years to come. The son of an acquaintance of Bess's, Dr. Merriweather suffered from a mysterious nervous depression - which seemed to ease somewhat when he engaged in lengthy conversations with Franc. They began to visit each other often and to exchange books. He was inspired to write a toast to her, having learned that her mother's family was indeed a First Family of Virginia:

> *Here's to that matchless superwoman*
> *The matchless FFB*
> *A truly modern daughter of the noble FFV*
> *A lineal descendant of those proud patrician dames*
> *Whose virtues so translucent*
> *Have glorified their names.*

It was not a romance but a new friendship that she greatly enjoyed. But along with it and the business courses that she hoped would lead her on a different path to independence, Franc still had to earn money. So she was soon back to nursing jobs, moving into an apartment building to care for the manager's ailing aunt. This experience was full of frustration as the patient complained a great deal, both at home in the apartment building with Franc and at the hospital where she had to go from time to time. The family seems to have expected Franc to clean the rooms - to do all the dirty work of housekeeping. She also seemed to be sewing for them. In the end, she noted:

> *I am in a terrible state, so disgusted with myself for placing myself subject to all sorts of grouches and acidity.*

Eventually, Bess brought her home and Franc was happy to be out of the "mess." But, she wrote in her code,

> *I am in another here.*

It is hard to know what Franc meant by that but the fact that she wrote it in code suggests there may have been problems in her living situation at the Burgies. Later on in the year, she mentioned instances that led her to feel that she had worn out her welcome there - but at this point, she says no more about it.

Fortunately, she had received a letter from a Mrs. Michener in Sumner, Mississippi, asking her to come there and care for her elderly mother for a short period. Franc accepted and in early December, made the 80 mile train trip to Sumner, a small town in the Mississippi Delta. Her time there reads more like a vacation than actual work. The 78 year old "patient" was easy to care for and Franc appreciated the large steam-heated home with its three servants and a laundry man. She was able, while there, to continue her writing, to go for long walks, to visit the Baptist and Presbyterian churches and to visit with the new minister and his family.

That job, of course, ended for Franc when the patient's daughter and family returned and on Christmas day that year, she wrote

> *Past (sic) the day among strangers in a mediocre boarding house. Gladys and J.L. came and brought my mail and took me to the P.C. (?) It turned dreadfully cold and rainy and blowy. Old man had lots of relatives come to see him.*

In January, she spent two days caring for a 19 year old mother who had just come home from the hospital with a baby boy and had a 14 month old girl threatened with pneumonia. Later in the month, Franc mentioned taking the Civil Service Examination but worried that she had fallen down utterly on the arithmetic.

Then there was a job in a "fine, big home" where Franc cared for an 81-year old woman who had a ruptured blood vessel in her heart. Franc found her to be a dear, sweet soul and a splendid patient but, after a brief period of improvement,

> *Waking from her nap, she said she felt very queer and began to be very sick....vomiting and gasping for breath. Sent for the Dr. who gave her strychnine but she was dead by 2:45 PM. It was a horrible death to see...I had to stand by and do the needful to the last gasp, then tie up her mouth..it was a terrible strain and ordeal. The family were good to me. One of the daughters put her arms around me and told me she was so glad I was there. They gave me $12 for two days and nights.*

A few days later, Franc traveled to Enid, Mississippi to care for a patient in a very different situation. The old man had had several strokes and was as helpless as a babe. Also, his reason had become affected.

> *It was a typical country house - discomforts, untidiness, conditions generally disagreeable...I was up, just as I arrived, all night. Then went over the hills and far away to get breakfast at a restaurant.*

A nephew was there but he was also ill. Others came to help but Franc did all the night work - while trying to study her arithmetic!

> *It is pretty tough and lonely - the night work. Everything is so cold - no fire in the dining room, none in the room I try to sleep in but my feet and legs cramp and I can't sleep. My feet and legs are swollen to twice their size.*

Finally she told them she would have to leave by the end of the week. But before she did, the patient began to fail and died the next day.

Back in Memphis, despite her plans to get into another kind of work, Franc met with various doctors. But before another job came up, Franc was sick herself and wrote that she had the worst day she had ever had. Everything ached - her head, throat, chest, shoulders, even her eyes. She wrote that she went to the Christian Science Church again but does not say anything about calling a "practitioner" to help.

She recovered, of course, and in late March, left the city to care for one of her final patients.

> *Got a call late today to go to Aloka, Tennessee, 35 miles north of here. I went and was met by a horse team and proceeded to drive for two solid hours - seven or eight miles from the station. Took a woman who lives near the patient. Stopped at Idaville, a little town two miles from the patient to consult with the Dr. He told me to just go and take charge of everything. He said the patient cannot recover - had measles - pneumonia-obstetrical combination and baby just 3 days old. I finally got to the patient. Being about 9/10 primitive, I could put up with the inconveniences and crudeness. There was no W.C. on the premises. Crude and simple and dirty and untidy in the extreme. Found the Dr. Brown quite a handsome and superior man - very nice and knows Dr. Merriweather. The patient passed on at 8:15. It was dreadful to see and hear the family. Dr. Brown took me home with him and I found Mrs. Brown very kind and hospitable.*

In Memphis with the Burgies again in early April, Franc hints strongly in her diary notes that it might be time to live elsewhere. She had been with Bess off and on for three years. The "children" were now young adults and tensions of all kinds were inevitable. On April 7th, Franc wrote that Gladys and J.L. and a friend were in a car accident.

> *They went over a bump full speed, bounced them so hard that ...Gladys' nose was cut. Mrs. Grooms came out and treated them. I had a terrible spell - found my tortoise shell comb broken and I made a remark about it. There was the very hell to pay. I nearly died. It was just the last straw and I was so miserable. Oh, God, deliver...*

Details are missing here but the long visit was clearly wearing on everyone's nerves. We wonder if Franc accused someone of breaking her comb - and if Mrs. Grooms was a Christian Science practitioner - and what the car accident had to do with the eventual "blow-up." Whatever the answers, Franc was clearly coming to the end of her Memphis visit. She began to push harder to finish the shorthand lessons and wrote letters to people who might recommend her for war work.

But then, in April, she got another nursing case. It was a 13 year old recovering from scarlet fever.

> *A palatial huge home away out at Overton Park...Everything lovely. Just have to read to her, play games such as Old Maid, Crazy Traveler, Pollyanna, Jack Straw - and model with colored putty. I sleep all night, take her temp 3 times a day, give a black pill at night and spray mouth and nostrils, bathe her all over every day.*

The patient was quarantined so Franc was a prisoner for the 3 weeks she was there.

> *But everything is so clean, comfortable and lovely and the view out over the Overton Park Golf Links makes the time pass pleasantly. The family are German Jews and they are notably lovely in their home life.*

After three weeks the patient was almost fully recovered. At the end, Franc spent a day disinfecting everything, assured that the house was fumigated, and was paid $75.00.

A couple of weeks earlier she had received a check for $350 from Wilfred Owens in Guatemala for sale of the Martinez house she had owned there. These two payments were a major influx of money for Franc and gave her the courage she needed to leave Memphis and the family for a time.

On May 7, 1918, Franc, armed with her new secretarial skills, headed for Washington to make the rounds of war activities. She visited several offices without getting any definite offers. But in the meantime, she was invited by a friend, Miss Mitchell, to come to New York for a visit. There, she wrote:

> *I was received with open arms and love......I cannot afford to stay but two weeks.*

Franc stayed for five years.

Chapter 20

NEW YORK! NEW YORK!

It was, perhaps, the perfect setting for Franc at this point in her life. There were plenty of outlets for her restless energy, people from every country and every walk of life to engage her interest, sights and sounds to distract her from her spells of grief and sadness. Family members and old friends appeared frequently in the city and kept loneliness at bay. Supporting herself financially was a continuing worry but in New York, the possibilities for work were far more numerous. There were restaurants to sample, movies to see, theatrical and musical presentations to enjoy and varied neighborhoods to explore. Her increasing interest in unusual religions and philosophies found frequent outlets. Of course, there were difficult times. Working in an office as a file clerk had its drawbacks. While this sort of work was an exciting new opportunity for many women at that time, it often placed them in positions that were subservient and open to exploitation. It is rather sad to reflect that this fearless woman who had shot pumas and rafted mahogany now had to become embroiled in petty office politics, worrying about misaddressed letters or going to lunch at the wrong time. But Franc took it in stride - more or less - and managed to prevail.

As soon as Franc arrived In New York on May 19, 1918, she was taken under the wing of Miss Mitchell - evidently an old friend, although I did not find any mention of her in earlier diaries. Perhaps she was a Monticello friend. Franc made contact quite soon with Rowland Ormsby and Marcello Rodriguez, friends from Guatemala and Belize days and both offered to help her find work. She and Miss Mitchell went on a sightseeing spree and, walking along the Great White Way with Marcello, Franc was sure she saw Jekyll! (Of course - she had not forgotten Guatemala - and her old enemy.)

Within the first two weeks, her nephew Howard, came to the city and was there for almost a month. They saw each other several times. Ormsby took her to a Spanish restaurant and she was "happy as could be" to be eating frijoles, chili and fried plantains again. She visited the "great unfinished Cathedral" - St. John the Divine - and made a trip to Long Island. Several evenings she stopped in at the Waldorf and sat in the lobby and listened to music.

And quite soon, on June 5 - less than a month after she arrived - she went to work as an office "girl" - filing, typing, etc. for $40 a month. It was in the office that Rowland Ormsby managed - importers and wholesale dealers in a variety of merchandise. Franc noted:

> *We got in at 7 and worked until 6. I like being in the office - there are 7 of us - 2 girl stenographers.*

Marcello also had an opening in his office which he offered her. A Mrs. McNeill phoned and offered her a job as nurse and "mother" at a girls school but Franc rather quickly decided to decline that one, suggesting that she was ready to be something other than a caretaker for awhile.

So she stayed with Row, though theirs was a complex relationship. Sometimes, in Franc's diaries, he comes through as the "heavy" boss, berating her for mistakes and threatening to fire her - but often, they spent the evenings together, dining and drinking or - later - visiting at his home with his new (third) wife, Madge. When Franc wrote about events in the office, she referred to him as Mr. O but describing their evenings together, he was always "Row." (Later, she had other, less endearing names for him.)

Marcello introduced Franc to his mother and sister, Mrs. and Miss Rodriguez. She spent a weekend with them at Rockaway Beach and it was the beginning of a lifelong friendship. She referred to them as "the Rods" and, throughout her New York years, she was in and out of their home continually and in later years, after she had left the city, made a trip to Mexico with them.

In July, Franc spent a day with the man who was to write several articles for <u>Field and Stream</u> about her. She had written to W. Livingston Larned when she was living in Miami because he had published an article about the King expedition in the Everglades in 1916. She wrote:

> *I feel I had a "finger" in that pie for I was their nearest neighbor and spent the night with the wife and their little daughter for the purposes of encouraging and sustaining their hopes.......I was there after their safe return just as I had felt would be the case and heard from the venturesome explorers something of their experiences, hardships and anxieties...*

She reminded him that she had written to him about her Central American experiences and that he had promised to write something up when it was convenient. Now, Franc wrote:

> *...the wheel has turned - I find myself ALONE in Greater New York, just one of the incalculable numbers of atoms that make up the human population here - not entirely from choice but, in part, from financial and mental necessity.*

Larned called her and invited her to his home:

> *He met me at the end of the subway at 242nd Street with his wife and children. They were perfectly lovely to me. Had two big pink gin cocktails, then ice cream, then a Scotch. Mr. Larned took notes as he asked questions - he is to write something right away. I got home about 1:30. Had a heart spell today.*

(Could it have been the pink gin?)

Back at the office, Row's affairs were a lively subject of interest. A woman named Madge phoned the office asking for him, and said she was at the Hotel Chelsea.

> *Row phoned Miss M at the office that they had gone straight to the parson! Ha, ha....Row brought her to the office..I received her into my open arms like a long lost sister. This is the* _third_ *one.....*

During the next few days. she wrote more about the lovers:

> *Mr. O supposed to leave today for his 'steenth honeymoon....*

> *They are back from the honeymoon and came to the office.*
> *Madge looks badly - skin and color awful.....Row was at the office*
> *awhile. Was as cross and impatient as a sore headed bear. They are*
> *over at Rockaway.*

Franc had known the first two Mrs. Ormsbys so she took a somewhat dim view of the possible happiness of this third attempt. However, she began to spend frequent evenings with them at their place in Rockaway - until that romance also ended a couple of years later and Madge left the city.

Where did Franc live in her New York years? There seem to have been several small apartments and/or furnished rooms but she doesn't mention the addresses. At first she was in a building with Miss Mitchell. She wrote about a traumatic event when a man who was working on an elevator was killed there. She also wrote about an actor who lived in the building and entertained them with tales of life on the stage.

But for Franc, being Franc, there was sure to be a romance somewhere in the offing. This time, it was with Hinajosa, a man in her office who began the flirtation by complimenting her dress and saying other sweet things to her. She responded by sticking his hand with her hat pen, then kissing it to make it well. This led to other kisses as they walked through the Park. But, like her other romances, it had its ups and downs. Between days at the beach and visits to movies and surreptitious hugs and kisses at the office, he went through spells of ignoring her. She suffered at his indifference and wrote several times:

> *Oh, God, please let me meet him tonight!*

But, calming down a bit, she noted:

> *He is the most erratic man - morose!*

And after suffering days of his alternating hot and cold behavior, Franc finally wrote:

> *Have not even thought of H this week.*

All we hear about him henceforth is office related - where he seemed to enjoy throwing his weight around.

Franc suffered more over a Burgie visit in September. Bess and her daughters came to the city and met nephew Charlie, who was on his way to fight in France and Bess's son J.L. came down from Toronto where he was in school. Along with Franc, they all went to the Palace Theatre and the Hippodrome. Then Franc had to work because the other office girls were off for the Jewish New Year, and the family carried on their fun without her. She wrote about this with some anguish, suggesting that, for all her activity, she was often quite lonely. She wrote:

> *I missed the folks so I went roaming around like a lost soul as usual - only ten million times worse - knowing that 5 of my nearest people were in town and I alone. Oh, how I suffered. Went out home and cried myself to sleep. Miss M came in about 7:20 and said the folks were at the Reading Rooms (Christian Science) so I went down - but I knew it was no use. I came right back. But they all came out after awhile. As I was washing the dishes, J.L. came to the kitchen and spoke to me. So we spent a pleasant evening together. I felt a lot better. Said goodbye to Charlie.*

Charlie left for Europe and the War. His mother, Sis, back in Kentucky, was sad and worried and wrote asking Bess to come to her. She did, and left Gladys, who was about 20 then, with Franc for a few days. Together, they went to the Waldorf for dinner, heard an entertainer named "Mitzie," and went to see Rector's Midnight Follies - a production that featured risque jokes and scandalous (for that time) curtain lines. Franc wrote - rather gleefully - that Gladys had her "eyes opened." (Was it safe to leave young girls with Franc?)

At some point while working for Rowland, Franc began to take an interest in Tameja again. Of course, she had not forgotten the situation down there but had managed to put it out or her mind and concentrate on making a living. But in Row's office, she heard people inquiring about land in that part of the world and wondered if there was any chance of selling hers. She began to try to get her papers from the Banco Americano. She got no response from them and finally wrote to Klanke, asking him to get copies for her of what he had. His answer was slow in coming and when it did, it was to tell her how expensive it would be to get the titles copied.

The war raged on in Europe - but Franc commented on it very little. She also said nothing about the suffragettes who were active at that time in their struggles for women's voting rights. In a way, this is surprising. She was an activist by nature, always wanting to get involved and make things better. It is hard to forget her bitter comments to Pat Bellingham about injustice to women and her vow to -

..go to any extreme to help women put it right.

Yet, at this point in her life, Franc's focus seems to have shifted to the practical, everyday business of making a living. All her energy was needed to arrange a life for herself that would be free from dependence on family and friends. In another letter to Pat, she had written:

I prefer freedom to anything else, even at the expense of pure poverty.

Unfortunately, by October, things were not going well with Row at the office. He had written a nasty letter that upset her and she began filling out applications at other places. She also moved her living place to an apartment on Madison Avenue. Hinajosa at the office was in the past as she began to talk about an Indian Prince who fascinated her and enthused over a Swedish opera singer she had met.

In early October, Franc was asked to go and care for a woman who had had an operation. She wrote,

So here I am just like old times.

But this must have been a weekend job as she remained in Row's office. She got a letter back wrongly addressed and Hinajosa berated her about it. She did not leave the office all day and skipped lunch. That evening she went straight to the Christian Science church on 96th Street where she stayed until after midnight reading the lessons. The next day, Hinajosa was at her again.

> *He rowed about a magazine I had in an envelope - said it had to be rolled - and a lot of nastiness.*

The following day, Franc wrote:

> *Mr. O called me in for consultation. I got there before the doors were open, then went to the P.O. They thought I was late - so I stayed late. Mr. O came back in and we had a talk. I told him the truth about some things. I made a mistake in mailing. I felt worried and nervous. I went to the C.S. lecture.*

These office issues, petty though they seem, were obviously of great concern to Franc as they threatened the job she needed so much to survive in New York. To help keep herself calm and strong enough to go on, she often went to the Reading Rooms or attended a Christian Science meeting or lecture in the evenings. In this diary entry, she seems to try to comfort herself with some of what she had learned there:

> *I am alone in the office between 1 and 1:30. All nonsense. We had an "indignation meeting" - we girls - for he said to Miss Gans "don't be so impertinant" when she said she did not stay out 2 hours at noon. And I said, "The office is never left and I always see that one of the girls is here before I go out." But it is as though it had never been. He cannot harm. We can only harm ourselves.*

A bright spot during this time of job anxiety was word from Larned that he was close to landing their article in <u>Field and Stream.</u> It was indeed published there, part of a series in which he called her "A Diana of the Jungle" and included tales of her game hunting, her fishing for sharks in the Golfete, her zoo in the jungle, and other stories of her life in Guatemala.

Franc spent very long days in the office but rarely went home to relax in the evenings. She went to meetings, had late dinners with friends and rarely seemed to get to bed before midnight. Her only day off was

Sunday and she often spent that sewing. Being well-dressed continued to be important to her.

Franc was in New York on November 7, 1918, when she experienced one of the great events of her lifetime. Four years earlier, she had stood on the grounds of the Forrester-Brown estate in Ireland and watched the troops parade to begin World War I. Now she stood in midtown Manhatten as it ended.

> *THE WAR IS OVER.*
> *Whistles began to blow and paper to fall like snow. It kept up until dark - downtown was the most marvelous sight in all history. One solid mass of whistling, horn blowing people and motors of every description. I am so thankful I saw it. Was in a movie picture taken from the Treasury steps. Our office kept right on with business.*

The 11th was the official peace day.

> *The whole city began its demonstration before day. Kept it up all day and night. <u>Such a demonstration the world has never seen and never will again.</u> All business stopped and closed after 12.*

In spite of problems at Row's office she continued to work there. Some days he would call her in and ask her how much she was making, then tell her it was not enough. Other days, he berated her about using the office phone for her calls. He would sometimes tell her to start looking for another job; then would invite her home for dinner with him and Madge and they would share a bottle. On New Year's Eve, Row called her into his office to scold her. In response, she wrote:

> *I took particular pains to wish him the best year he ever had.*

Chapter 21
DANCING - AND JOB HUNTING

Hopefully Row's New Year was better than Franc's turned out to be. Although she continued in his office until February, she spent at least half of 1919 unemployed and in anxious searches for a job. She began the year with her birthday on January 8, noting -

I have reached the half century mark!

She seems to have spent it alone except for a visit to the Christian Science church. A few days later, she tried a different sort of gathering - one of many alternative movements Franc would investigate in New York and later, in San Francisco. This one was the Church of the Silent Demand, led by a practitioner of the New Thought movement, Dr. Northrup. Franc wrote:

It was interesting and curious....All write on a slip of paper what they want "the way" opened for - then someone either audibly or in the silence "opens the way" to the fullfilment of your desire. I wanted the way opened in some line of work.

But apparently, it was not - or not just yet. In late January, she talked with Cleveland Moffatt, a magazine writer of note. He asked her to meet him and talk to a woman who wrote scenarios. France commented:

I found him a fine old fellow ...he wants to make a movie of my experiences.

But again she was disappointed and a few days later, wrote that Mr. Moffatt could not see her. He was ill - or had changed his mind - and we hear no more about a movie. (It could be quite wonderful, though - "Out of Africa" in Central America!)

Franc had still heard nothing from Banco Americano about her papers re Tameja and wrote to Klanke again in January asking him how much it would cost to get copies of his. She remarked that she had heard that Jekyll had died.

>*He is over there - across the Styx.*

Obviously, she could not imagine him in any other life-after-death setting!

Movie or no, property or no, Franc needed a real job prospect. Marcello asked her in February to take a nursing case and she did, although she seemed still to be employed in Row's office. The patient was a Mexican woman from the Yucatan whose family was important in the government there. Franc stayed with her at night and over a weekend, getting almost no sleep. The patient died, and on February 7, to no one's surprise, including Franc's she wrote:

>*Got a week's pay and 'passport' from Bailey Williams and Co. so I am free and on the hunt for a job. Did not speak to a soul on leaving. Mr. and Mrs. O (Row and Madge) went out without saying a word, for which I was very grateful.*

Franc went immediately to register at the Hirsch Agency and spent the next six months job hunting. She was relentless in her search. She answered want ads, traipsed the streets looking for possible openings and went on many interviews. Among the places she tried were: Salem Export and Import; U.S. Merchant Co; American Express; Wiggins-Wilmore; YMCA; Travelers Aid Society; Mt. Sinai Hospital; Askell and Douglas. She tried a "Hebrew place" to see about social work but could not speak Yiddish so that was out. She asked about working with addicts. Tucked into one of her diaries are yellowed want ads:

>*Typist for dictaphone work: instruction free, work simple and pleasant, salary and maintenance.*
>*Typists: high class, with good education for permanent positions; salary $15 to $18 (per day?)*
>*Young lady for filing and to make herself generally useful. Unusual opportunity for advancement. State age and salary.*

Franc tried for them all. And finally, for a short time in February and March, she worked at a job that seemed ideal for her and in which she seemed happier than at any time in years. It was one that she got as a result of volunteer work and contacts. She was a member of the University Club and she and other members had begun to visit soldiers and sailors at Bellevue Hospital. Although the war was over, these men were ill or wounded and not yet able to go home. Franc commented on her visits:

> *One was dying. Another one was from Venezuela of a fine, rich family in Caracas. He has fever. I talked to him in Spanish and said I would go to see his consul.*

On February 19, she wrote:

> *Mrs. Richards called me this AM and told me of the meeting of the ladies and that they wanted me to take charge of the social work of soldiers and sailors at Bellevue. I went down to see Mrs. R at the Univ. Club and got data for the work. They will pay $75 per month and petty expenses. Got $.50 cab fare ....really begin on Saturday.*

Fran threw herself into the job in her typical way, working long hours with men who were ready to leave the hospital. She found temporary housing for those with no money and clothes for those who needed them. She visited consulates and tried to arrange hospital visits and transportation home for men from other countries. She wrote:

> *I had a very good and full day at the hospital. Am more interested and content in mind than I have been in years. I love the work. So many interesting people and happenings...*

And on March 4, she was able to write:

> *Wedding Day. Forgot it! Thank God!*

Her happiness was reflected even in her dreams.

> *Had a flying dream last night - the very best I ever had - flew higher and with more ease - no effort..and I could light on a telegraph wire like a bird. It was marvelous.*

It did seem the perfect job for Franc - she could use her nursing skills, her experience with people from other countries and cultures, her Spanish language facility, her organizational abilities. And it must have been rather fun to have all those young soldiers to chat with. They were probably fascinated by Franc - younger men often were. But alas - on March 14, the month was over. She went to the hospital to turn everything over in good shape and wrote that she was treated very strangely - and was not paid. They took her name and address and said they would send a check but said nothing about her continuing to work. She wrote,

> *I left the hospital with a broken heart.*

It was a painful disappointment and one wonders, as Franc did, what went wrong. But she, resilient as always, went back to job hunting. She continued writing articles and decided to advertise herself as an interpreter and guide for Spanish speakers. Little came of that. She continued to go to the Christian Science church and attend lectures frequently. She spent quite a lot of time with the Rodriquez family - they often dined out and went to the theater. Friends appeared in town from time to time - she mentioned the Spencers, the Kings whom she had known in Miami, and Harry Ferguson whom she hadn't seen in 29 years! Row and Madge Ormsby also remained friends, in spite of her departure from Bailey Williams and their work association. The Ormsbys frequently invited her to their home, after which she sometimes wrote:

> *I had a lot to drink. Felt dreadful today.*

Later, she began to refer to Rowland as "Rags" followed by some unreadable words in her code and "Such a pity." But one day she met him on the street and went back to the Bailey Williams office with him. Everyone was cordial, she said, except "old henchaser" - her new name for her former paramour, Hinajosa. After one of her visits to them, the

Ormsbys told her they were going to have a baby. She continued to visit them from time to time and the child was born in October.

Franc's own family appeared in New York less often. When Gladys Burgie arrived there in May, she seemed to be occupied with other people and events and there was some difficulty in finding a time to get together with Franc. Gladys was bringing her some "cast off" clothes, Franc noted, and they finally met in Lord and Taylor. (No doubt, with the help of Franc's needle and thread, the "cast offs" would be recycled into stylish creations.) In June, her niece, Ruth and nephew, Charlie, visited and this was described by Franc in more satisfactory terms. They visited the Woolworth Tower and took a sightseeing boat at the Battery for a three hour trip around Manhatten. Fran said it was..

> *... splendid and wonderful and interesting.*

But she still needed a job! So she decided to take a new course in filing. It cost $30 which, she felt, was...

> *Awful! But I had to do something. I will then feel equipped for a dignified position.*

On June 6, she graduated from the class and got her certificate but a "dignified position" failed to fall into her lap immediately. After an interview at Askell and Douglass, she wrote:

> *They wanted a stenographer. I had a pleasant interview but that does not "make my baby a dress."*

Franc, at age 51, was competing with younger women for these clerical jobs, having started her career in office work after her careers as a plantation manager, diplomatic hostess, practical nurse, animal tamer and big game hunter - to name just a few. And of course, hers was a strong personality. Though potential employers must have found her fascinating and admirable, they may have feared she would be a disruptive influence in the docile workforce they would prefer.

She was discouraged but kept trying and managed to enjoy some summertime trips to the beach with the Rods. There was also a new man in her life - though all we know about him is that she called him "Irresistible."

Franc, around this time, began to hear from Jekyll's wife, Henrietta. Interestingly, she had never been mentioned in Franc's diaries in Guatemala. Jekyll might have been a confirmed bachelor, for all we knew. But with her husband gone, Henrietta seems interested in selling her part of Tameja and wants to see what Franc thinks about the idea and how much she might want for her part of it. They corresponded off and on for the next several years - though, thanks to Klanke's intransigence, they never succeeded in selling the property together.

On August 20, 1919, Franc got a call from the United Fruit Company - of all places! She filled out an application and the next day they put her to work. Her comment was:

> *Strange fate.*

Indeed it was! By that time, United Fruit owned most of the banana land in Guatemala, including her own former plantation. At their New York office, she had more supervisory experience than she had had at Bailey Williams and was in charge of 2 or 3 boys and girls who helped with the filing and other office work. She was to work Monday through Friday and on Saturday mornings - but being Franc, she often stayed at the office til 7 or 8 at night. She approached office work much as she had farm work in Columbus or sewing for WWI soldiers - she just kept at it 'til she was exhausted. This ought to have endeared her to her bosses - but clearly, it did not either at United Fruit or Bailey Williams. On September 4, she wrote:

> *I was told to go out to lunch before 2 - and not stay at the office after 5. Esta muy bien.*

Franc was paid $80 a month and in spite of the above directions from her employer, she wrote one day:

> *Did not go out to lunch nor even had a drop of water from breakfast to 8 PM.*

On Sundays, her one day off, she worked hard at home. She sewed, did laundry, scrubbed the bathoom, patched her own shoes, repaired an unbrella, fixed a corset cover and made her own hats. She also attended the Christian Science church at least once a week, went with friends to the beach, on sightseeing expeditions, to concerts and to dances. She commented:

> *I can't seem to get to bed before 1.*

Franc's nephew, Charlie, having survived the war and begun his lifelong work as an accountant, had married recently and the newlyweds came to New York in October on their honeymoon. His wife, Margaret, was a beautiful and talented young lady and Franc described their visit as follows:

> *They were here all last week. I only saw them once. Went up to the Penn Hotel o Friday 9th from the office. They had dinner with me - cost me $4.80. Then we went up to their room and they packed. Then, about 10:30, some cousins of M's came - naval men from La. where M is from. One had a girl with him and he introduced her as his wife to tease Margaret. We went to the Strand Roof Garden and had claret cup.....Margaret is a very advanced thinker, a decided individual, dainty as a piece of French china and as practical as can be. Makes all her own clothes...and was assistant to the head man in the largest auto supply store in the south, earning a big salary.*

Though complimentary, in a way, it is not a description that evokes warm feelings. And indeed, Charlie and Margaret's marriage did not last long.

In New York, as 1919 came to an end, Franc continued her large correspondence - which still included her dear friend, Lucy Potts, and her old Guatemalan servant, Agatha Miles - and continued to see the Rods often. With them, she spent an evening at a gala event at the

Penn Hotel where she wore a black evening gown made in Dublin thirteen years before. (That would have been the trip she and Will made in 1906 to meet his family. How the world had changed for her!) Another evening was spent at the Pan American Association where she met people who knew her friends in Guatemala and Belize. She began to attend lectures there and met more people from south of the border, enjoying it all immensely.

As Christmas approached, Franc was cheered by over 30 Christmas cards from her friends around the world. She listed them all in her diary. She even heard from an old friend about BZ, who was still paying the taxes on her Los Angeles property in Guatemala. She visited the Ormsbys, who now had a 2 month old baby, and helped finish off their Christmas turkey.

Enjoying the Twenties

Gainfully employed as she was and beginning to enjoy a busy social life, Franc approached her 51st birthday. It was the beginning of the "Roaring Twenties" and she was ready to be a part of it. In her diaries for 1920, there is more about dancing and dining and theatre-going than about long hours at work and visits to the Christian Science Reading rooms. In early January, she went to hear Caruso sing in *Aida* and noted that she had to pay $8.00 for a seat! On the 8th, her birthday, she suffered from a cold which became a more serious illness. She missed a day or two of work and had to persuade Miss Mitchell to call a Christian Science practitioner. She was reluctant and France noted,

> *We had a row about it first.*

Franc wrote that she did not really feel better until she was able to go to the Christian Science church. Then,

> *...that pain in my throat and chest that had me mad suddenly left me.*

A favorite place for dancing was the studio of the Countess Castle-Vecchio at Carnegie Hall. Franc went there in February and eventually signed up for an advanced class, ten lessons for $10. She wrote that it was the first lesson she had ever had even though she had danced ever since she could remember. After that, it was one dance after another for awhile: a Masque Dance at Club America; a big dance at the Penn Hotel with the Rods; a dance at Sadler's where she danced with "the Japs;" a dinner dance at the United Fruit Company Club at the Academy on 79th St; the annual affair and breakfast of the Dixie Club of NY at the Commodore. Other social activities included movies and plays and a meeting of the alumnae of Monticello Seminary. For the latter, she wore her "blue satin" and had a lovely time, naming in her diary all 30 of the "girls" who attended. At the theatre she saw Effie Shannon in "Mama's Affairs" and when nephew Howard was in town, they saw a show called "Shavings."

Franc continued to spend her free Sundays sewing. She referred several times to a burnt orange silk she was desperate to find but could not. There were some excursions out of town during the summer - to Bear Mountain, Sayville, the Atlantic Highlands. Addie Owens was in town for a visit with her husband but Franc's family seemed to be largely absent during this period.

Of course, Franc had not given up her appreciation for the opposite sex. She got a letter from BZ in May, telling her that he was paying the taxes on her Los Angeles *finca* and wrote:

> *He said not to worry about paying him back but it would be there if I ever came back. And he had "received many kindnesses up at the 'old house'." Sounded mighty good if it is true. Will send him a check.*

That letter must have warmed her heart and brought back memories both tender and exciting. But Franc's eyes were also on those males immediately around her. In July she went to a dance and wrote:

> *A darling little Chilean boy was there. Danced a lot with him. He does not know how yet. I am wild about him....he is handsome, God bless him. He is a student at Columbia.*

In August she seemed to fall hard for a person who came to see about a room where she lived. She called him "the Lion." Her description of their encounter is written in code - in this case, it is hard to decipher but was definitely "blissful." In September, she mentioned a Jere M - without further explanation. But having learned that he had just sailed for Santa Lucia, she experienced a sad and lonely evening.

> *I was feeling very ill and heartbroken again....I undressed and lay down. I suffered acutely with grief and loneliness...I got dressed again and walked down to the Rods. They were not in...they had gone to the Spanish Fiesta at Leslie Hall. I went up there and paid to get in - but could not find them.*

It was not long after this unhappy evening that she lost her United Fruit job. She had referred earlier in her 1920 diary to problems at the office. She had written an article about conditions there and entitled it "File Room Nightmare." It had been published in a trade paper called <u>Filing</u> and clearly, it did not endear her to her supervisors. In July, she wrote:

> *Feeling very ill and blue and discouraged over incidents in the office. Very bad treatment by Mr. B.*

Franc also had a fall at work. Standing on a stool while filing, she toppled over and hurt her left arm and ankle. It was quite painful for a few days. And finally, on September 12, she wrote in her diary, "Red Letter Day:"

> *Went to office and was told that Mr. Balshering wanted to see me. He just simply informed me that they could get on without my services in the file room - and said I could go to the cashier and get my pay to the end of the month. There was great consternation among the many friends I had made there. I was telling the others about it when Mr. B followed me and told me not to speak to anyone. He could not have been viler. I went into the Ladies Room and all the girls came in and we had a great powwow.*

Franc had worked at this job for a year. The Bailey Williams job had lasted less time than that and between the two, there had been 6 months of unemployment. Now she faced another discouraging period of job hunting. Though we have few specific details about happenings at her offices, she was obviously an energetic worker. There is no indication that she was incompetent. She seemed quite willing to come early and stay late. But this could have been a threat to her co-workers and even to her bosses, whose work ethic may have paled in comparison. She may have been perceived as insubordinate. As we know, she was opinionated and not likely to stay quiet about anything she considered an injustice. She probably did not fit in as one of an office full of clerical workers who were expected to docilely do as they were told.

After losing this United Fruit Co. job, Franc was at the Filing School the very next day, hoping for a temp job to tide her over. One was available immediately. However she decided to a take a bit of a vacation and went with a friend to live in a tent on the St Lawrence river for two weeks. While there, she lived in a house boat some of the time and met Norman Rockwell's wife who was staying nearby. When she returned to New York, she began a temp job and continued working at those for the remainder of the year.

Franc had a shock in the Fall when she discovered that her old friend, Livingston Larned, had published an article using some of the material she had given him without asking her permission. She was angry and wrote to him; his answer, she wrote, was a "rip snorter." He accused her of ingratitude and their friendship suffered for several months, although the rift was eventually repaired.

Chapter 22
MEDIUMS AND MESSAGES

As 1920 drew to a close and her jobless financial situation preoccupied her, Franc says very little about dancing and shows. Instead, she seemed to become more interested in spiritualism. She wrote in October that:

> *I went to the Spiritualist Church of Advanced Thought and I had a sweet message from my darling. He appeared in evening dress. I was much affected.*

Through this interest, she met a couple named Hinson. They began to attend seances together and she and Mrs. Hinson started a course on the occult led by a man named Dinshah. Franc referred to him as a "brilliant scientist" and seems to have been entirely captivated by him for awhile. In her diary for 1921, his name is mentioned over and over and it is full of notes and quotations from his lectures. It is hard to say what his philosophy or religion was - there seem to be elements of eastern religions and mysticism and Christianity, She made notes in her diaries - "history of the earth," "earth in the present epoch." It is hard to make much sense of it all from the brief notes she made but she was heavily involved in these thoughts for several months.

Even as Franc plunged into this new enthusiasm, she also entered another period of great anxiety about finding work. She had seemed rather cavalier about it after she lost the UFC job and was apparently managing with temporary work - jobs that lasted a few weeks, or even just a few days. But by mid-December she began to visit agencies daily and was sent on numerous interviews. Some were wild goose chases. Most employers seemed to want younger types. There were promises to call her back - or let her know - but then they didn't. She wrote in early January:

> *I was at rock bottom of the slough of despair!*

The Zitreen agency raised her hopes when they sent her to see a movie man, Mr. Rubenstein, who planned to send her down south (to the Caribbean) with a camera man. She was elated and wrote to Larned to try to retrieve some of her photos which he had. The job fell through - but the correspondence with Larned was a step in repairing their relationship. Before long they were friends again and happily sharing pink gin cocktails.

Franc was encouraged by one of her agents to look at magazines that might publish her articles or at least use her material in some way. She thought of her old friend, Jeff Davis, a journalist she had met on one of her trips to Guatemala and was now in Washington. She got in touch with him. He promised to see her when he was in New York to visit his fiance and she eagerly anticipated that. But he did not call. Franc wrote:

> *It upset my whole day. There is no chance. I am horribly upset.*

But there was nothing to do but keep trying. Of course, she continued to see friends - the Rods and Row and Madge were ever faithful - and she still danced - and still attended Dinshah's lectures on topics ranging from customs of India to earth in the "4th round." And a pleasant surprise was a visit with Robbie Hempstead, a friend from Guatemala days who gave her news of old acquaintances and continued to see her from time to time when in New York.

But the relentless job hunting was exhausting. One day in Feburary, Franc noted that she felt all in and after getting her supper, lay down and was not able to get up. Of course, the next morning she did but instead of returning to the hunt, she went to Mrs. Hinson's and she wrote:

> *I followed the line of least resistance - just couldn't help it. I went with Mrs. H. to take the dog for a walk along Riverside - all the way to Grant's Tomb. Sat awhile to rest - the weather was wonderful. Went over to Amsterdam to a market, then to Alexandria.*

That night they went to Dinshah's lecture and Franc wrote that he ranted and raved as expected - on love - justice - judges - etc. (She seems not always to have taken him entirely seriously.) After this little respite, she felt better and was able to take up her search again the next day. It went on - with visits to the editor of <u>World Travel</u>, to the Weaver Agency, to the Central Fire Company, to the Ford Agency.

Her interest in spiritualism increased through the year and occupied most of her non-working - or non-job hunting - time. Looking at this 100 years later, it is not easy to understand the appeal of these practitioners to a woman like Franc - well educated for her time, practical and hard working as well as fun loving and possessed of a highly developed sense of humor. Perhaps if she were still grieving Will - but it had been ten years since his death and she had moved on. Getting in touch with him beyond the grave does not seem to be a burning motivation for her visiting mediums. But she was always interested in new ideas and movements and spiritualism was something of a fad at that time. Interesting people she knew in New York were engaged in it and she was curious. Whatever her motivation, her diaries for the remainder of her time in New York are full of her experiences with mediums, seers, psychics, and swamis.

On March 14, Franc went to the Occult Center and later in the month to see Mrs. Helen Wells, a spiritualist, automatic writer and artist who was active in the Ethical Society. Franc wrote that it was an interesting evening -

> *Mrs. Von Buskirk gave some "messages" - saw marvelous drawings.*

On the 20th, she went to a meeting of the First Church of Animal Rights at the Astor Hotel and on the 20th, to hear Ransom, a practitioner from London who had been in jail.

In April, Franc went to a "message" meeting with Mrs. Lochman and the next day, to the All-Cult Medical Assocation. There she heard Dinshah again, talking about "so-called incurable diseases." But her fascination with him was coming to an end. She noted that at a meeting in late April, he..

> *..was on a rampage and turned a man out in a peremptory manner, then launched into a harangue about giving up the classes.*

When she went to hear him again, she wrote:

> *We got nowhere. I think we have seen him for the last time. I am more sorry and disgusted than I can say. I will miss the meetings very much.*

But there were others. She went to the Astor to hear lessons from Harry Gaze and paid $10 for a course of five lectures. She also went to a spiritualist on W 67th St. who had his own church and wrote:

> *Several very good mediums were there. Said there will be a change in my life in the Autumn.*

Franc went back to Mrs. Wells and looked at her automatic drawings again. On May 8, she heard a professor from China at Town Hall, sponsored by the Theosophical Society. On May 17, she heard Baron Eugene Ferson from Russia talk about the "Triune Harmonial System." On May 27, she was at a spiritualist meeting on Broadway and wrote:

> *The medium gave me a symbolical message from my darling around his seal ring. Said there was a circle with electric bulbs, all but two lit. These two would soon be lit and then all would be a complete bright circle. The medium said I did right to keep the ring in my possession and not let them have it over there.*

(Over there? Ireland?) At the Church of the Holy Spirit in June, the medium said he saw a blue light all around her. But he could tell her nothing specific. The next day at a Christian Spiritualist meeting, she again learned nothing. Then she went to John Smith's church. He was a spiritualist and medium and....

He said my husband was there and said a lot of things purported to come from him that sound just like him.

On February 28, 1922, a Mrs. Forest told her..

My pathway will be strewn with flowers very soon.

Franc often jotted in her diary notes from the various lectures and meetings she attended. From this period in her life, there were such bits as: Karma after Life; the Voice of the Suicide; Proof of Incarnation; The Flame of Life; The Path of Discipleship - Yoga; the Path of Discipleship - the Chela's Sacrifice.

But of course, she had not given up dancing. On March 12, she went to a dance at the Waldorf and on the 17th, to a fancy dress event where she wore a costume fashioned of posters and stamps related to a famine in China.

Franc in the Chinese famine costume

She had been working at a temp job for an organization that was raising money for this. But she wrote after the party:

It was very original - but no one appreciated it - didn't seem to know there is a famine in China!

But of course, she had fun anyway and danced in her stocking feet til 4 A.M. She had her photo taken in the famine costume and sent it to the Memphis <u>Commercial Appeal</u> where it was printed in April.

It is hard to tell where Franc was working by this time because the jobs were all temporary. She was still anxious to find something permanent and continued to fill out applications and visit agencies but wrote in June:

There is nothing doing. Much worse than in winter.

She continued to submit items to newspapers and magazines. On March 21, the <u>Angler</u> paid her $20 for 15 illustrations and data. <u>The Brooklyn Eagle</u> agreed to publish her brief article called "The Strategy of the Ants" which explained how they strip fruit trees and then protect themselves. In November, she received a copy of <u>World Travel</u> which included her article, "Up the Rio Dulce and Beyond" but was puzzled as to why the name Graham Gaylord was on it along with hers. It was an article in which she had written about visits to churches and other historic sights in Guatemala City and Antigua. She knew nothing about him and seems to have gotten no answer to her queries about him. (He was probably a recognizable name to the magazine's readers and added to encourage them to read the piece.)

Franc's old friend and employer - and much married man - Rowland Ormsby appeared on the scene again in June of 1921. She had gone by the Bailey Williams office and learned that Row was sick. On the 21st, she went over to Jersey to visit him and found him in..

..a fearful state. I knew my place was here so was up with Mr. O all night.

She got him into the City Hospital in Jersey City. She noted that "George" had come home but it is not clear who he was - a son by an earlier marriage, perhaps? But Madge, Row's current wife, was not there. Instead, she was in London and there was discussion between Franc and George about whether to notify her - which suggests that they were separated at this point. Obviously, Row was unlucky in love - or perhaps his wives were.

By the end of June, Row was comatose. Franc was called at 1 AM on the 30th to the hospital. She wrote:

> *He passed into the Astral at 1:30 AM. I stood close to him and watched the passing and advised the others and then hunted the nurse on duty.*

He was buried in the Jersey City cemetary. Few people came to the funeral and no money belonging to Ormsby could be located. She wrote that his office would not pay for anything - and that Hinajosa was especially "nasty and hard" about it. This experience must have saddened Franc, though her relationship with Row had had many ups and downs. He had been a steady tie to her life in the tropics. And there were all those dining and drinking evenings in New York which must have had their bright moments - along with the "morning after's" regrets.

Lucy Potts was in New York for a visit in September. Franc was greatly cheered by her visit and when she left, Franc wrote:

> *I miss her.*

Whatever was going on in Franc's life, it was important to her to look well and, at this point - at age 51 - it took a little more effort. She still weighed herself often and was sometimes pleased, at other times, horrified. She was no longer a slender girl. But she was still a handsome woman and dressed well, continuing to make her own dresses, coats and hats. One day she wrote:

> *Stayed home all day and did a lot of odd things. Put mud on my face.*

On July 24,

Dyed my hair. It was a frightful job. Could not go out all day.

On June 26,

Wrote for a chin strop. $2.00

(Think what she would have done if botox had been available!)

Looking for a permanent job continued to occupy her but the Filing Association usually had temporary work available. As Christmas approached, she received cards and notes - from "darling Felix" and others. But she didn't mention Christmas Day or her birthday in January of 1922.

Franc continued to visit mediums and attend meetings. In February, she wrote about a wonderful evening at the "Circle Lafayette" to celebrate Washington's birthday at the Waldorf.

A grand collection of distinguished, talented people - a Russian and French countess, a Scottish chief of three clans - fine singers. It was the best thing I have been to.

Her 1922 diary stopped rather abruptly in March when she wrote that she had been to a dance:

Went up and danced and was lucky and danced every one.

It was a happy note with which to end Franc's time in New York. When we meet her again, she will be heading west.

Franc in 1924 in San Francisco

Chapter 23

GOING WEST

There could hardly have been a more fitting spot for the next stage in Franc's life journey than San Francisco. Where else would she have found such a variety of esoteric societies, alternative religions, psychic practitioners, eastern mystics – and dance halls. The weather was better and the scenery of course, spectacular. In her three years there, she was involved in a mind-numbing array of activities: the Theosophical Society, the Spirit Church, New Era Expression Club, Gita classes, Raw Food classes, Hindu temples, the Spiritualist Temple, the Psychic Research Society and the Hobo Movement - to name just a few. But before settling into west coast life, there were some detours along the way.

We are not sure just when Franc left New York. She noted when she began a San Francisco job in January of 1924 that her last job had ended a year and a half earlier – September, 1922. The next diary we have found begins in the summer of 1923. It seems likely that she remained in New York for several months after that last diary entry in March of '22 and must have been considering what her next step in life would be. She had been without steady work since mid-1920 and we have seen that, after a number of disappointing interviews, she had settled for short-term jobs.

Had Franc ever, through these years, thought of returning to Guatemala for a visit? Could she have managed it financially? A letter to Franc from a long-time correspondent in Guatemala in February, 1923, indicates that she had considered it. Agatha Miles had worked for Franc intermittently for much of the time Franc lived in the tropics – as housekeeper, cook, and in other capacities. Theirs seems to have been a close but occasionally rocky relationship, with Agatha being easily offended and not always available when needed. Franc mentioned her off and on in her Guatemala diaries but she did not seem to be a constant presence.

It is hard to tell what ethnicity Agatha was. She mentioned Belize rather often and seems to have visited there frequently while working for Franc. She was articulate in her letters and expressed herself clearly, but was not highly educated. She seemed to see herself as a "servant" but was not an Indian or a Carib and her name suggests some English blood. There was a suggestion by her executor, nephew Charlie, that Agatha was Jamaican. At any rate, after Franc returned to the States, they corresponded regularly and that continued until Franc's death. She saved many of Agatha's letters which were always full of news and gossip about people Franc had known in Livingston and the vicinity and were full of affection for Franc. She always ended them "Your old servant" or sometimes "Your true and affectionate servant." In February of 1923, she wrote Franc that she had found a room for her in Livingston at the hotel, and that the owner would let her have it at a discounted rate. So evidently, Franc had seriously thought about a visit at that time. Agatha was very glad that she was coming but cautioned her that she would not find Livingston as she had left it. She wrote,

> *It is quite different.*

But Franc did not go to Livingston. In June of 1923, an article about her appeared in Denver's <u>Rocky Mountain News.</u> She was visiting a cousin, en route to the Pacific coast. After writing about Franc's life in the jungles and her other travels and referring to her as now a well-groomed society woman, the reporter wrote:

> *She was planning to return to the tropics when she suddenly decided to take the western trip and visit her old home here. From Denver, she plans to go to the Pacific coast, locating there for awhile.*

And so…. Franc's next diary begins there in July, 1923. On the 22nd, she wrote, presumably in San Francisco:

> *Duffin is in town and we met. I phoned that I was going to Olympia in the AM. Hurried to Ina's, parked everything, left my trunk to be sent…Got to Olympia at 9 PM and came right out to Mrs. Kent.*

Olympia

Several questions arise. Who was Ina? Who was Duffin? Who was Mrs. Kent? We can surmise that Ina was the person who urged Franc to come West. Perhaps she was a relative on the Martin side of the family. Perhaps she was a friend from Monticello days. Duffin is also something of a puzzle as he is rarely mentioned in earlier diaries. Franc refers to a Mrs. Duffin in her Memphis diaries from years before so maybe he was her son. Occasionally, in her New York diaries, Franc mentioned that Duffin was in town but without further explanation. But in this case, she seemed to be in Olympia, Washington, for two months at his invitation and much of her time was spent with him. It was a period of pleasure and relaxation without any attempts to find work. She boarded while there at the home of Mrs. Kent, to whom Duffin introduced her.

Franc and Duffin's relationship that summer was odd – perhaps "complicated," to use a current phrase. They went for frequent drives in his car and he often took her to his golf club or to movies or to visit friends. He also took her to his office to meet his coworkers. But she found his behavior puzzling and commented about it from time to time:

> *Duffin rather glum and scarcely spoke to me*
> *Duffin came home, then left right away for vacation. Said adieu in an indifferent way. Like an iceberg – but I will not melt him – though I am sure I could.(!)*

On a drive in August, she had to drag every word out of him by questions. On another drive, she wrote that he was silent as a tomb:

> *He is so exasperating. I can't stand it.*

Even so, it was not a romance and Franc did not appear to be in love. There was no "suffering agonies" when he ignored her as had happened with other men in her life who became distant. Her reactions were often more amused than sorrowful, especially after some of their frequent drives.

> *Went for a drive with Duff – got lost and did not get back til nearly 12. Ran out of gas. It was exciting and fun.*

Duff was apparently an erratic driver. One night after a movie and drinks at the Elks Club, they..

> *..smashed the hub cap on his car – left it downtown and walked home. When I thanked him for the day, he just said, 'That's alright.'*

Another drive ended in a ditch, from which they had to be rescued. After a drive to Aberdeen in August, Franc wrote:

> *We had a few little mishaps but wonderful demons of divine protection.*

Sometimes Franc and Duff were accompanied by a Miss W, with whom Duff "clashed in grand style" while Franc looked on. At the golf club, Franc enjoyed sitting in the shade and reading and writing while Duff played. There were also picnics and other events where she met some delightful people, including the governor of the state.

When she was not with Duffin and his friends, Franc cared for Mrs. Kent when she was sick and also made some trips to sights nearby. She visited a Mrs. Emmons on Day Island in Puget Sound. She took a boat to Seattle and had a bus ride around the city. In Tacoma, she had an interview with a reporter at the <u>Tacoma Times-Tribune</u>. She had sent him something she had written but instead of publishing it, he wanted to interview her and asked her to give him a photo. On September 3, it accompanied a long write-up with which she was quite pleased. The article ended, quoting her:

> *The jungle life was fascinating, in its way, and I was very happy there. But I have told other women that the only thing that made it possible and endurable for a white woman would be a real love of nature and a great love for her husband. It is not the manner of life that naturally appeals to a woman.*

To say the least! Overall, this summer in Olympia seems a lighthearted respite for Franc after her recent intense years in New York. She had embarked on her time there six years before with high hopes and excitement, thinking it would be just a visit. Then, deciding to remain awhile, she had enjoyed some unforgettable pleasures such as only that city can offer and had made some lifelong friends. But she had endured difficult and disappointing work experiences and had exhausted herself in efforts to find jobs to keep her going. Christian Science and spiritualism had been her comforts there. As she settles in San Francisco, will they continue to sustain her? Or will there be something new and different to satisfy her curiosity and consume her restless energy? This summer of her 54th year had been a time to play, to relax, to get ready for the next chapter in her unusual life.

San Francisco

We have mentioned a few of the activities that filled Franc's life in San Francisco and it is hard not to notice that many of them expressed her continuing attraction to Eastern religions and philosophies as well as to psychic phenomena and spiritualism. But a new, quite different interest began to consume her in early 1924. It was the Hobo Movement, a serious effort in the 1920's to help homeless men who moved from city to city looking for seasonal employment. We often think of them as tramps who roamed the highways and hopped freight trains carrying their possessions in a sack over their shoulder. Organizers of the movement attempted to find places for such men to stay in various cities and provide a community where they might socialize and educate themselves. There were even "hobo colleges." Chicago was a particular center for the movement. When one of the organizers arrived in San Francisco and got in touch with her, Franc threw herself wholeheartedly into the effort to start a "local' there. While it may seem a complete departure from her somewhat other-worldly interests of recent years, it was a resurgence of her lifelong interest in helping the less fortunate, reminding us of the morphine addicts in Miami, the Associated Charities in Memphis, the many sick Guatemalans she had cared for.

But first – Franc needed a paying job. In November, 1923, she wrote:

> *I have continued to follow every lead I could think of – but it*
> *seems hopeless.*

After trying General Electric, U.S. Steel and the Emporium and going to the National Association for Women's Service and the 10% Agency for help, she wrote:

> *I learned that when they advertise for a $75-$85 file clerk*
> *it meant they wanted some 'flapper.' Not very encouraging but I*
> *know there is a place for me. So 'I should worry.'*

Clearly, she was trying to practice positive thinking and not lapse into despair. She turned down an offer to teach Spanish in exchange for a room and also an offer from a jeweler. About the latter she wrote:

> *I refused. 8:30 to 5:30 including all day Saturday is against*
> *my principles. Miss Hall from the Agency called and advised me*
> *strongly to take it for several reasons. But I can't see my way – have*
> *thought about it from all angles and continuously – but will not*
> *take it.*

But though she was not working, Franc was rarely idle. She spent her time in San Francisco much as she had in New York. She investigated the city. She walked along the wharfs, up Nob Hill, around Chinatown, through the parks and squares. She attended classes and lectures and club meetings and religious ceremonies. And she still loved to dance. A favorite spot was Gordon's, which she described:

> *There was a huge dance floor where the butcher, the baker*
> *and the candlestick maker all danced. I saw my shoemaker there.*

One evening at another hall, she danced with a nice young fellow who told someone that...

> *...he liked waltzing with me more than anyone he had ever*
> *waltzed with. I loved it. I am mad to dance.*

Franc began to attend the Theosophical Society in November and learned about its founder, Madame Blavatsky, a world traveler who had developed her philosophy based on an Unwrittten Secret Doctrine she believed underlies all religions. But there was also the astrology class which Franc attended on Mondays and "Raw Food" class on Tuesday, and the "Gita" class on Saturday. Raw Food was evidently a fad at that time - and periodically has a resurgence - because of beliefs, among other things, that cooked food contains harmful toxins and raw food contains enzymes that aid digestion. "Gita" is, of course, the shortened form of Bhagavad Gita, the sacred scripture of Hinduism. That led her on to visiting Hindu temples - such as the Swami Prakashananda - and going to lectures by an Indian named Chatterjee on several occasions. And there was the New Era Expression Club which sponsored lectures, including one by Alice Craig. Of her, Franc wrote:

> *She was forceful and perfectly groomed. Talked on the "unkissed woman and the unkissable man." (!)*

Franc always made friends easily and soon developed a regular circle of companions with whom the visited the sights of San Francisco. They went to Golden Gate Park and the Cliff House and visited the ship Intrepid. She mentioned Mrs. Hamm, Mrs. Baruch, Miss Jones and Mr. and Mrs. Eggar. And after a day of sightseeing, she often stopped at the St. Francis Hotel where she sat in the lobby writing letters.

Through Gita class, she became friends with a lecturer there, W. Goldschmidt. On November 12, he walked her home and they talked for a long time. The next day he came for tea and she wrote:

> *I enjoyed it so much. He is an interesting type. I think I have his "number."*

Whatever that may mean, it doesn't seem to be the beginning of a romance. She began to help him with the distribution of a periodical he published called "Broadcast," addressing wrappers for it and even taking work home with her. One night he came to her place and told her all his domestic troubles.

He has a wife in Los Angeles. Left her in a temper. They may be divorced - I didn't get it all.

But a day or two later, Franc was repeating an all-too-familiar scenario. After a lecture he gave on the "Migration of the Races" at Gita class, Goldschmidt didn't speak to her. The same thing happened two days later and she wrote:

He sure is moody.

Her first Christmas (of 1923) on the West Coast approached and was a happier holiday than other Christmases of her widowhood - which she had often spent alone in rented rooms or in the homes of patients she cared for. On Christmas day, she took fruit to Mr. and Mrs. Eggar who had recently arrived from Canada and had no money or work yet. Miss Jones brought a turkey and Goldschmidt was there also. She wrote:

We had a happy day together - all strangers in San Francisco and "homeless."

Franc noted on January 11, 1924, that her 55th birthday had passed unnoticed. However, she did not express any particular sorrow about this and seemed contented (or as contented as her restless nature would allow). She had spent the week with her classes and lectures and dinners - and of course, dancing. She had been to a club where Chatterjee and other Hindus were and where she saw Goldschmidt "actually dancing." She wrote that she had taken up a collection in Gita class to give him a nice briefcase to carry his plunder in.

And, having settled into her new environment and made these new friends, Franc finally got a job! She wrote on January 10:

I was sent to the Aetna Fire Insurance Co - they said they would take me. I went in to say I would take it. Very small salary - $70 per month - but I decided to take it to start.

She wrote little about the job but seems to have stayed with it for the next two years.

Hobos

In February of 1924, Franc embarked on her new enthusiasm, the Hobo Movement. James Eads How, the founder of the International Brotherhood Welfare Association, arrived in San Francisco and he and Franc met for dinner. They had corresponded briefly before he got there although it is not clear how their connection came about. How was the heir of a wealthy St. Louis family, his grandfather having built the Eads Bridge there. Early in life, he seemed determined to give all he had to help those less fortunate. He got a degree in theology, studied medicine, joined the Fabian Society, and attempted to found a monastic order. Eventually he concentrated his energy on work with hobos, using all his money for that purpose and living a life of near-poverty. He founded the IBWA, which was a sort of union for hobos and included hobo colleges, hobo jounalism and conventions of hobos. When he died, at only 56, one of the causes was starvation; he truly had given all he had.

After their dinner together, Franc began to serve on a committee to find meeting places for the group in San Francisco. She organized the first hobo meeting there at Liberty Hall. She had invited a number of people whom she had met through her lectures and club meetings - especially through the New Era Expression Club - to show support for the hobos who were expected to attend. Unfortunately, only 5 men came. She wrote:

> *I was sick and ashamed over it, after asking all the people to come - but I am sure we will make a "go" of it next week and Mr. How and others will help.*

The following week, she tramped around for more than 4 hours looking for a place where the IBWA could meet regularly. After a long day of looking at halls, going to a movie with a friend, talking with a blind man in the hotel lobby til 11:45 and doing her wash, she wrote at 1:30 AM:

> *I am woefully disillusioned - but see the good and beauty anyway.*

(A little more rest might have helped.) However, things looked up a few days later when she was visited by Leon Brown, a man who had been a hobo and had been helped by the IBWA. He had become prosperous and gave Franc a contribution of money. He also offered to help her get the local going. She finally found a hall for the next meeting and again invited friends and fellow club members. The meeting on March 27 was a great success with a full hall and 50 signed application forms.

Having helped to launch the Hobo Movement in San Francisco, Franc continued to attend meetings and help plan events. In May, there was a hobo dance where ice cream and soft drinks were served. It went well and two more dances followed. However, the third one was a "fizzle," according to Franc, and she noted that How went home offended. Evidently, drinking was involved. She wrote that they would have no more dances - but the meetings continued and Franc always attended along with a few other regulars whom she called the "Boes." She continued to see How at these meetings. Sometimes he went home with her. But there was no suggestion of romance - How, with his ascetic, almost monastic lifestyle, was probably not a candidate for flirtation.

Franc's interest in spiritualism continued. At one visit to the Spiritualist Temple, she asked the medium about her and Bess's immediate future. She was told that there "will be tears." Gladys had written to her that Bess was in bed and must stay there for three weeks due to high blood pressure. Worried about her, Franc went to visit a healer who was called the "Wonderman" and while he performed his ceremony, she kept Bess in her thoughts. She also had a reading done by a Mrs. Oakdale who used the science of numerology.

Franc had a disappointing experience with a new friend in April - one that seemed to cause her real pain. Miss C had been invited to stay with Franc for a time at her hotel. But one day, having left her still in bed and gone shopping, Franc came home to find her gone, leaving a cold note with no forwarding address or phone number. She wrote:

> *It was such a slap in the face I could not eat a mouthful. I was quite upset - and felt so strange. But I will just forget it.*

It isn't clear why Franc found this so painful. Perhaps, in spite of all her activity, she was lonely and liked the prospect of having a companion for awhile. She referred sometimes during this period to someone she called "Lover" who lived in the same hotel. Once he called when she was asleep and said he was alone and asked her to come up. She insisted that he come down instead - and he did. What happened after that will have to be left to our imaginations - as we have left details of other encounters with men. There always seemed to be one about - somewhere.

But loneliness was usually kept at bay. Along with her hobo meetings and lectures and seances, she even attended "rousing" meetings at the Mission where she enjoyed singing - hymns! Shades of her Protestant past! Can she have been belting out "Onward Christian Soldiers" one night and visiting a medium the next? In Franc's case - yes. She still loved dancing, going to such halls as La Vero or Sadler's or Dean's. She attended a Hawaiian dinner and watched hula dancing. She met a wide variety of people and commented on an evening with a gay couple:

> *I went to dinner with Patzner and his man friend. There was another lady there - friend of a friend. A very good dinner which Patzner prepared - just a salad composed of 13 different things and then tomatoes filled with cottage cheese and raisins - very good.*

As Franc continued her involvement with all these clubs and societies, her comments about them were often more amused than impressed. In August, she commented that there was an "almost fist fight" connected with electing new officers at the New Era Expression Club. She wrote:

> *It was more fun than I have had since I came to San Francisco.*

After a meeting of the Psychic Research Society, she wrote:

> *Jesus Christ was there with some of his Pentecostal followers. He is the longhaired, long bearded, barefoot old man who does not believe in bathing and he is a sight. But he is a fine height and physique with good shaped head and feet. One of the Pentecostal sisters went under the power of the Holy Ghost and spoke in unknown tongues, then translated the gibberish in English.*

Such comments suggest that she may have become involved in these esoteric societies as much out of curiosity and for their entertainment value as a serious effort to find inspiration and meaning for her life.

Thoughts of her Guatemala land had not disappeared entirely and from time to time letters arrived that brought it to mind again. Henrietta Jekyll wrote that the house at Tameja had fallen down and suggested they let Captain Owens try to sell the *finca.*. BZ wrote that he was paying the taxes on Los Angeles. Her friend, Lucy, had sent Franc the data to prove she still owned Los Angeles and Franc wrote her:

> *Seems a pity that with all that land - Tameja and Los Angeles - that I can't manage some sort of income from it. I wish I could come down next spring. I am trying to work it out but it is hard to save on my income....I would love a taste of the old times again, to go to another ball in the City. I try to dance twice a week here. I feel so wonderful after dancing a few hours, especially if I am very tired from a hard day at the office.*

But there was no immediate prospect of such a visit and Franc went on with her San Francisco life. She was always eager to learn and, in the fall of 1924, she began to take a university extension course in writing feature stories and syndicated columns. A feature she wrote on the mahogany business was published in the <u>San Francisco Daily News</u> in November along with a photograph. She got to work on an article about the banana business and wrote:

> *Our teacher said my story was <u>very good</u> and with a little change it would be a <u>National Geographic</u> story. I was delighted.*

Christmas approached and Franc got cards from many old friends and relatives whom she noted in her diary. But she wrote nothing about how she celebrated the holiday, nor her birthday on January 8. In February 1925, we find her at a Hobo meeting at a new and better venue, along with the other boes, and attending a lecture on healing by talking to the superconscious mind! As the year wore on, these activities and others similar continued.

But she also talked about hearing by "babygram" that her great niece Carol Porter (Ruth's daughter) had been born. She received a "fine, dear letter" from her old friend Larned and was able to visit with a son of the Kings, her Florida friends. A couple of Monticello "girls" came to see her. And she continued her longtime correspondence with Lucy. By this time, Lucy was nearly 80 and had finally sold Jocolo. Her most recent Guatemalan news was that BZ had married! (What had happened to Lola - the wife we knew?)

And other Guatemalan news began to come more frequently. A man named Miguel Medina wrote to Franc, saying that he had planted bananas on the Tameja property and requested her permission (after the fact) to continue to do so and to collect money from the other squatters there and send her the rent. She gave him permission and designated Agatha as her contact person to receive the payments. She also asked Agatha to try to clarify what the status of the property now was, especially with regard to Klanke's claims. In answer, Agatha wrote that Mr. Reed (the consul) gave her a slip with this information:

> *As an Industrial Partner of the company which was known as the Tameja Fruit Company, Mr. Klanke claims 1/3 interest. The affairs of the company were never liquidated. Mr. Klanke says the company owes him a certain sum of money and as a protection, he embargoed the place. The case is still pending in the courts of 1st Instance in the Department of Izabal. In order that his rights and interests may not suffer, he sees to it that the taxes on the property are religiously paid.*

So - little had changed in ten years.... Agatha urged Franc not to worry.

> *As you know, Mrs. Brown, poor weak women cannot go with men to fight against them for they are much stronger.*

Of course, Franc had never thought of herself as a poor weak woman and was not about to do so now. Neither was Henrietta Jekyll who continued to write to Franc, wishing she could get down to Guatemala even though she could not do anything with "those crooks." She wrote:

205

> *You had no business saving that Devil Klanke's life. Nobody*
> *wants to have anything to do with Tameja because of his claims.*

Franc also heard from Medina's brother, Isadore, who told her that Miguel had died suddenly and he and Miguel's widow, Felicia, would like to continue the arrangement with her regarding the bananas. However, Klanke had appeared on the scene and was insisting that the rent money go to him.

Still sewing.... This one's odd!

And on and on it went. But Franc's busy San Francisco life continued and as always Franc had a few notes about her clothes - an ever fascinating subject. This time, instead of sewing, she seemed to be dyeing. A friend, Mrs. Hardy, was helping her to spruce up her wardrobe by redesigning and changing colors. She added pieces of silk to a black coat dress and dyed a coat and some dresses. Franc helped her and also paid her $6 at one point. She enjoyed this activity as she always seems to have enjoyed fashion - although this dress is a bit odd...

The lure of exotic societies and new ideas continued unabated. Franc began to attend lectures by a Dr. deDanville who was a "he/she" and dressed as a man. He advocated drugless methods of healing, including Dinshah's (didn't we leave him back in New York?) altered color waves - spectrochrome therapy. Theosophy meetings continued - she made notes on the "Phases of Intentional Knowledge."

In September Franc went to a dance where she met a Russian, Victor Nascedkin. She did not immediately fall into ecstacies over him but merely says a month or so later that ....

> *...he has been attentive.*

She began to write about him often and to go to events where there were other Russians - a big family dinner, concerts. One night she went to a Russian ball with him but seems to have come home from it with a different man - Mr. Jadovsky. They sat in the park til 2:30 and she wrote in code that he kissed her and it was wonderful. But Nascedkin remained attentive and when her birthday came on January 8, 1926, he and her other Russian friends sent gifts.

But in March of that year, Franc's diary entries ceased rather abruptly. Within the next 3 or 4 months, she moved to Memphis to be with Bess. A letter from Lucy Potts in September 1926 is addressed to Franc there and hopes that her sister is better.

Franc had seemed happy in San Francisco with her clubs and classes and sightseeing and her eclectic assortment of friends. Her job seems to have been stable - she wrote nothing about problems in the office and there were no threats she might lose it. The Russian, though she enjoyed his company, does not seem to have thrilled her in quite the way the "Lover" or the "Lion" had - but at age 57, perhaps she was less apt to walk on air - with anyone. She seemed calmer, less anxious. She did not write about spells of nervousness that drove her out to find a Reading Room or an event to distract her. She even had some renewed hope that she could realize some income from her properties in the south. She was in a good place.

Bess, however, was her closest sibling. In age, they were less than two years apart and grew up together, even attending Monticello at the same time. When Franc came back to the States after Will's death, Bess had welcomed her with open arms. Her home was Franc's as long as she needed it and when Franc lived in Miami and later, in New York, Bess could be counted on for financial support when circumstances became dire. For many reasons - not the least of which may have been Franc's natural inclination to care for the sick - she would have felt that her place was with Bess when her health began to fail.

Chapter 24
THE TRAVELER

The next diary we have begins nearly a year later and covers a 6,155 mile "road trip" - Memphis to San Diego. Franc was accompanied by her niece, Frances (Bess's youngest daughter who was about 21 at the time) and two young men, Joe Payton and John Graham. She was considerably older than the other three so perhaps her role was that of "chaperone." She noted in her diary that they were riding in a Buick Sedan and that they left Memphis on January 4, 1927.

It was a long trip, especially for that time, when cars were slower and mishaps such as flat tires and engine malfunction occurred frequently. But some days they covered as much as 300 miles. Franc wrote about the hotels they stayed in - some quite nice, some without running water - and the food along the way which, though cheap (lunch cost $.75) was often not very tasty. They made it to Dallas by the second night and spent two days with her nephew, Eugene Pennebaker (Sis's eldest son) and his family of six children. Bess and her older daughter, Gladys, met them all there but then returned home to Memphis by train. Franc and the other three drove on to El Paso - where the fun really began.

On Franc's 58th birthday, they crossed the border into Juarez and played roulette at the casino there. She wrote that she thought of her birthday the year before in her San Francisco studio with her Russian friends. And she remembered the last time she had been in Juarez - 32 years before and married just three days! The four visited several casinos and finally walked back across the border to their hotel where they danced into the night, Franc evidently having a glorious time while the much younger Frances gave in to fatigue and went to bed.

Franc en route to San Diego, 1927

Then it was off to Douglas, AZ, then Tombstone, then Phoenix, then Yuma where they again crossed the border - in search of Mexican food. After leaving Yuma, they were stopped by a policeman for speeding and fined $10. Franc was quite annoyed with the other three over this incident - not so much because of the speeding but because they wasted so much time arguing with the policeman. She stopped writing in her diary very soon after this and we learn no more about the trip.

There are no diaries for the remainder of 1927 but it appears that Franc went from San Diego to Los Angeles and spent some time there before returning to Bess's home in Memphis. There are copies of letters Franc wrote from there, continuing to deal with Guatemalan issues. One of them is to the Vice-Consul in Guatemala City in which she requested a formal report on her properties. When she received it, it confirmed what had already been stated numerous times: It was subject to litigation due to the claim by Klanke that he was entitled to 1/3 ownership as remuneration for his managerial services. He was the Industrial Partner and in Guatemala, the Industrial Partner was favoured.

He can with no expense keep this in the courts for years.

Even so, Franc wrote to Henrietta Jekyll that she had met a man in Los Angeles who seemed interested in the property. Not hearing from her, she sent several more letters. There evidently was a real estate boom in Los Angeles at that time - money was being easily made and Franc was terribly frustrated that she had nothing to invest in it.

But learning that Bess was still far from well, Franc returned to Memphis and was there when she died on January 27, 1928. It was a sad event for Franc and in letters to Agatha and the Susans and other friends, she talked about how much she missed her adored sister. She felt at loose ends and unsure where she would settle or what she would do.

We have a letter dated February 6, 1928, from her nephew, Charlie, who was the executor of Bess's estate. Bess, along with her three children, was heir to the Burgie Vinegar Company which had remained a successful enterprise after Jeff's death in 1914. So Bess was financially quite comfortable and did not forget her sisters in her will. To Sis, she left two interest-bearing bonds. To Franc she also left bonds - but also shares in the vinegar company which would pay periodic dividends. Franc would have an income of about $75.00 a month. It was not a fortune but at that time in history, she could manage on it without having to find work. It must have been an enormous load off her mind after her years of struggle and financial anxiety. She would be free to follow the call of the open road, visiting friends and relatives and seeing new sights along the way. And, indeed, her life spanned the continent for the next eight years.

But Franc's home, her permanent address "where I can always be reached" became the Pennebaker farm in Kentucky. Franc spent summers there in Columbus for the rest of her life. Sis and Charles were aging and farm work was hard. Franc was determined to help them out in the busy farm season. And, as indicated in several letters she wrote to her nephew Charlie in '29, she also wanted to help them move from the farm into town. She was concerned about what she perceived as the "drudgery" of their lives and the small amount they were earning but was afraid that Charles would never agree to move.(And, in fact, he never did.)

Franc offered to cash in some bonds she had to help them pay for a home in nearby Clinton - though she noted that she herself could never live there! Small town Kentucky life did not appeal to her even though she was happy enough to help get them through the summers.

Through it all, Franc's correspondence concerning Guatemala continued in fits and starts. Klanke seems to have reappeared at Tameja and was insisting that all rents be paid to him. Franc was using the services of her old friend Pablo Doerscher to insure that the rent money from Miguel got to her so Klanke felt it was important to explain to Pablo how their business difficulties had come about. He wrote a long harangue giving his version of it all and sent copies to Franc and Henrietta Jekyll. In this document, we learn that Klanke had a long time intense hatred for Jekyll whom he accused of trying kill him at one time. He perceived Will as a weak man duped by the "devil Jekyll." He wrote:

> *I could renounce my sacred rights but I must not because what is right is right and what is wrong must be righted and if Mrs. Brown and Mrs. Jekyll think they can walk over me, they are sadly mistaken....My duty is to protect what is mine.*

As if that tirade was not sufficient, a few months later he wrote a separate letter to Henrietta Jekyll stating many of the same complaints. Of course, he sent Franc a copy. In a letter to Henrietta, Franc wrote:

> *...I have tried to banish the whole thing from my mind for I desire peace of mind above all else and would not begin a rehash of all that Tameja muck if I never got a penny out of it.....Klanke sure expresses a good opinion of himself. He sure has as good a "forgettery" as anyone I ever knew. It may be good that he can forget the terrible depths to which he sank when he was "in his cups" - forgets the dirty work I did with my own hands after one of those "depths."....It does rather rile me when he assumes the ABUSED role, making out he was so terribly wronged. I guess he really believes it....*

Agatha continued to write Franc and to try to keep an eye on the squatters at Tameja. She could do little but continued to express her great affection for Franc.

> *Yes, Mrs. Brown, you are a very good and kind lady to us all. I could never forget you. You are always in my mind. ...you were always so good to me.*

To Henrietta, Franc wrote in October from Sis's farm:

> *I have been buried here in this isolated spot since the first of June. But I have enjoyed being with my own kinfolks and I like the country except in the winter. I am getting homesick for the bright lights and the things I love about the city....Don't worry over Tameja or Klanke. ..Whatever happens it will be as it should be. Nothing comes to us but our own - be what it may. We must have "sown" it somewhere, sometime or it could not be "reaped." Such is my fatalistic idea.*

Years of Christian Science reading, visits to mediums, lectures on Eastern philosophies and just living - did it all add up to "whatever will be, will be?"

Sometime in 1929, Franc made her way to Chicago and resided at an apartment on Woodlawn Avenue. But there is no information available about her life there. What motivated her to go? Who did she know there? If she kept a diary, it has not been found but she commented on Chicago winters in one of her letters to Charlie:

> *...we have had continuous winter - rain, sleet, snow and everything caked with ice, like glass. So difficult to walk since January 1st and every day around zero or below. Some say we have already had more winter than they had all winter long last year. I don't stay out very long at a time, tho I do go out every day - just to walk. We are too far from the loop and it costs so much in car fare for me to get down there very often - tho I would love to be down every day.*

So why was she there? Of course, she loved cities and the excitement they offered - and Chicago offered much, as New York and San Francisco had. But it sounds far from an appealing place to spend the winter. So the following year, Franc returned to her old stomping ground, Miami, and very sensibly spent the next two winters there. We do have diaries for those years - 1930-31 - and know something about her activities, which were constant, varied and exhausting to contemplate. But except for these two diaries and a few letters, we know little about the last five years of Franc's life.

In Miami in 1930, Franc stayed initially with Lucy Whitman, her old friend from Guatemala days. We first heard about Lucy back in 1907 when she was newly engaged and visited Franc at Tameja. Franc, being slightly older, became her "confidante" and they corresponded through the years.

This might have been *deja vu* for Franc, who surely remembered her time in Miami in 1915-16 with Lucy's mother. Those were exceptionally hard years, for she was still grieving for Will and trying to support herself by nursing morphine-addicted patients. 1930-31 would be a very different story.

In fact, these diaries for 1930-31 read a bit like the San Francisco diaries for 1925-26 in the number and variety of activities Franc pursued. But instead of hobos, Gita, theosophy, and spiritualism, she was now involved in such "mainstream" groups as garden clubs, women's clubs, the Civic Club, the Town and Gown Club and the League of Women Voters. She went to the theater often, to outdoor band concerts, to lectures and to the country club. She also played hand after hand of bridge. Her life there was a constant round of activities. Lucy was engaged in her own pursuits, including teaching a Spanish class and acting with theater groups. Franc, in Miami, lived the life of a society clubwoman as she accompanied Lucy to dinners and concerts, and on excursions to the Everglades and the Singing Tower at Lake Wells and to Indian reservations. It was almost a throwback to her "bright social career" of the 1890's in Denver - as if Guatemala, New York and San Francisco had never been!

Franc was more than pleased when, in Miami, she was able to make contact with another old friend from Guatemala days. That was Addie Owens, the daughter of the American ambassador there. Addie had been a young woman then, unmarried and, like Lucy, looking to Franc as her older friend and confidante. After meeting again in Miami, they spent a great deal of time together. There was an interruption in their contact when Addie's husband died suddenly and she had a breakdown which necessitated a period of rest in a Retreat. Of course, visiting her there and being a sympathetic ear was just Franc's cup of tea and she visited often, taking flowers and gifts. After a few months, Addie came out of the Retreat and they were often together, Franc taking Addie to the theatre and to club meetings, the Washington Irving Society being a recent addition to Franc's collection of interests.

But there was, as always, great variety in Franc's enthusiasms. One day she mentioned swimming, on another it was a health lecture, on another a lecture on the Workman's Compensation bill that was being discussed in Tallahassee, on another a lecture on "laws for women." There was also a meeting of the All-Message Circle (so she was still going to seances!) and visits to clubs that were promoting good will and feeling between U.S. and Latin Countries.

But spending the summers in Miami was a no more appealing prospect than icy winters in Chicago. In May of 1930, Franc began a round of visits with relatives: niece Frances in Atlanta, nephew Howard in Greenville, South Carolina, Sis at the Columbus farm, Martin relatives in Tennessee, Howard again in Hattiesburg, Mississippi, then as Christmas approached, a few days in New Orleans with her nephew Eugene's family.

After these visits, Franc retuned to Miami and continued to enjoy the company of Lucy and Addie. They were young and energetic and Franc enjoyed the role of continuing to be a sort of mentor to them. She continued with the clubs and lectures and meetings and general social activity in Miami. But in May of 1931, her diary ended rather abruptly and no more diaries have been found. She apparently headed for the Pennebaker farm again to spend the summer. We have a letter from her nephew Charlie written in October of 1931 thanking her for taking good care of things at the farm while Sallie and Charles were away, including "putting the old buggy" in shape for them - and anticipating her return the following summer.

Wherever Franc lived in the winter months, letters from her Guatemalan connections continued to reach her. In 1931, she began to hear from Henrietta Jekyll's daughter, Grace, who seemed to have a buyer for Tameja. But as usual, that came to nothing due to Klanke's intransigence. Franc wrote that he was there and having everything his own way whereas..

> *I am hard pushed to eke out an existence and especially now when the meager income I have been trying to manage on has been reduced in various ways.*

The Depression was causing hardship at every level - Bergie Vinegar stock was no exception.

In March, 1933, Franc began to hear from Klanke's wife, Marie, who suggested that if Franc was not really interested in keeping the Tameja land, she (Marie) would buy it. She had some money of her own and was making this offer without her husband's knowledge. She offered $1,000 in three installments.

Rather surprisingly, Franc agreed - Klanke's wife! But she was truly ready to be rid of Tameja - and needed money. However, she wrote to Marie that she still wanted to keep Los Angeles and hoped to visit there eventually. So she sent her power of attorney to A. Arathoon in April, giving him the right to handle the finances of the sale. But of course, all was not smooth. How could it ever be in that environment? Money from Marie did not arrive for awhile, then came in small increments. In August, Marie wrote, saying it was due to the "terrible money depression."

In December, Marie said that Arathoon had sent a check for $125. Franc did not get it and noted that Arathoon was no longer in Livingston at the Legation and that another payment was due. Klanke wrote saying his wife had been very ill. In September, Marie wrote that it had taken a long time to get the case through the various government offices and that expenses due to her illness had been heavy. In January, 1935, no money having arrived, Franc received the following from Marie:

> *I owe you money and am sorry indeed to disappoint you. What has happened is that we borrowed money for the coffee plantation (at Los Angeles). We could not keep up the payments and the bank has taken it.*

Whether Franc ever received any more money from Marie Klanke, we don't know. It is more than likely that she did not. After 25 years, loud arguments, visits to judges, endless *escritos,* thousands of bitter words, and very little money changing hands, Klanke had won Tameja, after all....

A letter from Franc - written in March of 1934 - tells us that she was in Mexico with her old friends, the Rodriguez family, the "Rods" who had always been there for her in New York in good times and bad. They were in Mexico for several months and Franc wrote a letter to the family on hearing of her brother-in-law Charles Pennebaker's death:

> *Dad has been in my life like a dad since I was quite young and still very childish... Yes, Sis and all of you have been fortunate indeed to have had him so long - an eternal inspiration for all who knew and loved him for his 'beautifully lived' life, as you express it, Ruth.*

She envisioned the farewell at the Columbus church and all the people who were there.

> *But I simply could not have held up under it all. I am so sensitive and emotional...if I could have done the first thing to help, I could have arisen to the occasion but knowing that his devoted children were doing all that was humanly possible, I can excuse my absence.*

Franc went on to offer financial assistance if needed and promised to go to the farm and get the house ready for Sis. That she did and was there in May when her nephew Howard and his family - wife Lila and their children - came to spend two months with Sis and Franc. When they left to go to South Carolina, hoping to re-settle there, Franc wrote to Howard, sending a check so that he could have an operation he needed. For someone who had experienced so much financial uncertainty during her widowhood, she was extremely generous with family members. But in the letter she wrote to him, she said,

> *...be as grateful as you like for the DEED but not to the PERSON...*

She also urged him not to tell a soul about it! Franc's letter to Howard from the farm in September, 1934, is long and chatty, full of details about life on a Kentucky farm where there was not a lot of hired help.

> *The end of my day's work is driving the young chickens into the small hen house where they have roosts in the winter. They had been roosting in the trees near the stable in the orchard and under the shed where the vehicles are but now when they hear me whoopin' they begin to scamper and some go to the house...*
>
> *The jobs never end - soon it will be firewood, coal, ashes, in and out. I had all the chimneys cleaned and everything is now in readiness for the stoves, except the enameling of the pipes which I aim to do tomorrow....*
>
> *..the days are not long enuf to get all the daily jobs that crop up done - unexpected things take so much time - yesterday I had to rub up the new harness. Today it was shelling butter beans - picking turnip greens leaf by leaf and washing them, then I had to climb to the loft for a sack of cobs for kindling the fire.*
>
> *The yard is my fancy work - I get at it when I can - the moles have burrowed every inch of the yard this end of the grape arbor... Old John caught a mole the other day. I slit it across between the hind feet and skinned it like pulling off a glove, saving its front feet and its skull, so it is perfect. I filled it with bran after putting lime on and it is in fine shape.*
>
> *.. am sure Sis wrote you about selling Maud and then of her tragic death just a week after she left here. I sure grieved over her leaving and her death, tho I believe it was for the best for she may*

have been mistreated and made to work hard in her old age. We sure miss her - I kissed her goodbye.

Franc was back at the farm in 1936 when Sis became ill and was taken to the Gartley-Ramsey hospital in Memphis. She wrote to Charlie and Howard that she was dealing with the farm chores. Her muscles were stiff and sore from hoeing, spading and planting. She wrote Howard about the abundance of cherries and quoted the hired man, John, as saying:

I sure wish Mr. Howard was here to help me pick. He could climb the tree.

And there were the chickens, the radishes, the asparagus that had to be cut clean every day.

In June, Franc wrote to Charlie about preparing for Sis to come home from the hospital.

You speak of having "Maybelle or someone come early every morning to get breakfast and help get her started for the day." Don't quite understand - just where am I expected to be when she comes home? Up until last week, she seemed able to get up when she felt like it and I always had the fires in the stoves all laid, ready for a match and the kettle on the stove. I always said at night, "now call me when you wake and I'll get up and start the fires and get you and breakfast ready" - which I did and can do again.

And so Franc did - for the rest of her life. But that life would not be much longer. Sis came home from the hospital but was still not very well. Franc cared for her and continued to manage the farm but in early August, 1936, Franc herself contracted pneumonia. She was taken to the Dunn Hospital near Clinton where she died on August 13. She was 67.

Three days later, Sis died at Ruth's home in Clinton - the house where Franc had hoped Charles and Sis could enjoy a peaceful old age. A double funeral was held for Sallie and Franc at the Columbus Baptist Church. In the obituary in the local paper, it was noted that:

> *Mrs. Brown's most outstanding characteristic was her charitable spirit and her unselfishness. Her greatest joy in life was making the way more pleasant for others.*

It was a quiet, almost obscure end to a life that had been so full. Perhaps it was rather fitting that she whose father was a Baptist preacher was buried from a Baptist church in the South. Yet religion of the traditional sort had not figured very large in her life for many years. Whether she had continued to be a Christian Scientist, I am not sure. She seemed always to be seeking answers to life's questions, trying to find them with Mary Baker Eddy's writings, or Dinshah's lectures, or at a medium's seance. But she was not a contemplative sort; movement and activity were more likely than deep thought to define her personality.

The obituary was typical for funerals then - and was true enough. But we could argue that it makes her sound a bit saint-like which, of course, she was not. We have seen the fascinating contrasts in her - the "9/10 primitive, born savage," the seamstress, the farmer, the artist, the animal tamer, the dancer, the loyal friend, the spiritualist, the loving (though frustrated!) wife. But perhaps the obituary was right in in its emphasis on her "making the way more pleasant for others." Franc was doing when she got sick what she had done so often - caring for someone who was ill. As she had done for Rowe in New York, for Jeff and Bess in Memphis, for many of all races and classes in Guatemala, she dropped everything and went to care for Sallie. It was ironic that she - the younger sister, the caretaker - died first but appropriate that their funeral was shared. We can easily imagine a kitchen table somewhere in "the astral" where the sisters are still laughing at having just turned over a glass of tea for the third time.

Afterword

Franc's will indicated that her heirs were the four Pennebakers (Sis's children), the three Burgies (Bess's) and Hudson Strode, the son of her deceased brother, Tom. Charlie Pennebaker was designated as her executor and within six months of her death - in February of 1937 - he made a trip to Guatemala to have a look at Los Angeles, the only property she had clear title to at the time of her death.

Charlie was accompanied by two of his friends and he wrote an enjoyable account of their journey through Mexico, visiting Cuernavaca, Taxco and Mexico City. From there they went by train, crossing the Guatemalan border and arriving in Guatemala City where they were met by Franc's friend, Arathoon. The next day they met Klanke. Then they received a call from Jekyll's brother George and were entertained by him at the American Club. He told them that Klanke didn't own any interest in Tameja.

Here we go again!

But by the time they left the country, having visited all the tourist sites as well as the Los Angeles *finca* and Tameja (where they noted that Mrs. Klanke lived, in "an attractive thatched roof, dirt floor, native type house, very cool and comfortable") they had transferred the titles to Franc's heirs and arranged for the taxes to be paid on Los Angeles each year. Charlie kept meticulous records and saved every tax receipt - which amounted to less than $3.00 a year.

The property on the south shore of Lake Izabal seemed to be worth almost nothing at the time - the banana disease had been devastating and squatters farming on the land simply eked out a living as best they could, paying little rent. As the years passed, family members continued to hope that it would become more valuable. There were rumors that oil companies were interested in drilling there and Charlie investigated that thoroughly in the '50's. That came to nothing and even if oil had been found, the government had already mandated that the owner of the land would get little of the oil money. In the Sixties, there was the prospect of nickle mining in the area - but it turned out to be some distance away from Los Angeles. Yet - hope remained.

Charlie died in the late Sixties and I have no information about whether taxes continued to be paid - or whether the Guatemalan government eventually took the property due to non-payment. I leave it to some youthful family member to investigate and perhaps continue the saga. This story has been about Franc and I shall leave it there, hoping that you have come to admire and appreciate her, as I have.

Acknowledgments

The material I have used to write this story has come primarily from diaries, letters and other memorabilia which have been preserved by Pennebaker and Porter family members.

I want to thank my late cousin, Philip Porter, and his wife, Louise, for preserving all the memorabilia kept by Phil's mother who was Franc's niece, Ruth. She lived nearby in Clinton, Kentucky when Franc died and kept all that was found in Franc's possession at her death in 1936. When Ruth died, about 20 years ago, Phil kept it and shared it with me. He also researched some of the Strode family ancestors and gave me the information he had found.

I also want to thank Judie Pardue, my sister, for caring for the material concerning Franc's Guatemala years. Franc's nephew, Charlie Pennebaker, was her advisor with regard to financial and legal matters and was, at her death, her executor. He kept all the papers and documents regarding Los Angeles and the ledgers in which she had recorded the events of their life there. He had no descendants and these materials were left in his home in Memphis at his death. Judie was living in Memphis at that time and in the course of visiting his ailing widow, was able to retrieve these documents just before they were thrown out with the trash. Judie has cared for them since then and shared them with me.

Thanks also to my nephew, John Pardue, for "cracking" Franc's secret code so that we could learn things we might not have known otherwise. These "secrets" help bring her alive for us as we see the complicated, interesting human being that she was.

And thanks to the other descendants of Franc's nieces and nephews who have shared their memories of her or remembered their parents' remarks. These include Eugene and Bill Pennebaker and Mary Wikstrom, grandchildren of Sis; and Jo Barton, grandchild of Bess. Jo remembered that Franc was once known as "The Queen of the Central American Jungle."

Glossary Of Terms Often Used By Franc

Aduana   -   custom house

Alcalde   -   mayor or chief burgess of the town

Boats:

     Pitpain   -   a long, flat bottomed canoe, used in the streams of the banana fincas

     Dinghy   -   small boat carried on or towed behind a larger boat, as lifeboat or tender

     Tender   -   a ship that serves other ships, may carry passengers from ship to shore

     Lighter   -   large flat-bottomed boat used in loading and unloading ships

     Launch   -   small motorboat that is open or has the forepart of the hull covered

     Steamer   -   a ship that is propelled by steam engines

Escritos   -   official papers - deeds, titles to property, etc.

Finca   -   a plantation

Heradera   -   a written proof of inheritance

Jefe   -   a chief. Used to refer to the head man of the area, not necessarily the mayor

Mozoes   -   boys, fellows, workers around the plantations

Picetes   -   narrow overhanging jungle trails through the mahogany forest

Triste   -   sad, dismal, gloomy sorrowful. A French word used often to describe her state ofmind

Wipili   -   sometimes spelled huipil. A loose fitting tunic usually woven by hand on a backstrap loom. Colorful designs are woven into the fabric - usually done by Mayan Indians.

Articles Written By Or About Franc

I. Published Material

With Rod and Gun in a Mahogany Camp - by Livingston Larned and Frances Forrester Brown. <u>Field and Stream</u>, nd c1920

A Diana of the Jungle. 4 part series by W. Livingston Larned, <u>Field and Stream,</u> c1919

> "Stocking a Plantation Zoo"
> "Plumed Meteors of Guatemala"
> "Big Game Hunting in the Quiriqua Ruins"
> "Fishing in Guatemala"

Up the Rio Dulce and Beyond - by Graham Gaylord and Frances Forrester-Brown, <u>World Traveler,</u> 1921

Gathering Mahogany in Guatemala - by Frances Forrester-Brown. <u>The TropicMagazine,</u> nd

Article from the Denver <u>Rocky Mountain News</u>

Article from an Olympia, Washington newspaper.

II. Manuscripts by Franc, unpublished

Romance and Courage in Bananaland San Francisco, c1924

A Jungle Menu New York, c1919

Emergency Rations Memphis, nd

Traveling Experiences nd

Cameos of Tropical Travel Miami nd

Jungle Manna: a personal experience San Francisco c1924

Mahogany, Romance, Adventure San Francisco, c1924

Frog Intelligence New York, c1919

The Non-Reversable Von Kluck (a poem) Miami, c1915

Article on Caribs. New York, nd

About the Author

Sara Richardson is a great niece of the subject - Frances Forrester-Brown. She was a Librarian for 20 years and has been a Tour Professional in Philadelphia for 15 years. She has an M.A. in History from the University of North Carolina at Chapel Hill and an M.S. in Library/Information Science from Drexel University. She is the author of <u>The Methodist Experience: a History of the Methodist Hospital School of Nursing</u> and miscellaneous article and reviews. She has a son and daughter and three grandsons and, though a Southerner by birth, has lived in Philadelphia for 45 years.